W9-ACX-077

Poſtern gate

The Towre
of London

NDON

the time of
ck Cade's
surrection

Beere howſe

Battle bridge

Horßey downe

LORD OF LONDON

LORD OF LONDON

ERIC N. SIMONS

FREDERICK MULLER LIMITED
LONDON

*First published in Great Britain in
1963 by Frederick Muller Limited.*

*Printed by
Tonbridge Printers Limited,
Peach Hall Works, Tonbridge,
Kent.*

*Photographs in this book are reproduced by kind permission of; The
Radio Times Hulton Picture Library, The Mansell Collection, British
Museum and John R. Freeman.*

Dedicated to
PATRICIA, SUSAN, LESLEY and
MARGARET

CONTENTS

CONTENTS

ILLUSTRATIONS

Introduction

HISTORY is of little importance to the ordinary reader unless both he and the historian find it exciting. In this book I have taken a fragment of medieval history and tried to infuse into it some of the excitement it aroused in me.

The first Shakespearean play I ever read was *Henry VI, Part II*. Nine years old and at a Christmas party, I became bored by the noisy horseplay of the bigger boys, and detecting a book on a side table, opened it at random and, young as I was, lost myself completely in the story of Jack Cade, until an adult, convinced that I was reading merely in desperation because no one was making enough fuss of me, insisted on my participation in some game or other.

I must have understood and enjoyed that play, because I came away insisting on being given by Santa Claus a copy, all for myself, of Shakespeare. I got it.

I am ashamed, however, to say how many years passed before I read that play again, but when I did, as an adult, I was disappointed and unconvinced. It seemed to me unlikely that the son of a bricklayer, a 'clothier', a 'sheep-stealer', could ever have won so great a following as to frighten the King of England. So I began to delve deeply into his history, and grew steadily more excited.

Cade was, I discovered, a man of mystery and his story full of tremendous human interest. After reading all I could of his life and times, I felt that this was not enough. Some of the truth concerning his career could be approached only by personal investigation. So I finished up by setting off, rucksack on back, to tramp over most of the country and through many of the towns concerned in his rebellion.

On the way, I turned aside here and there to examine this local library and that. Some yielded small, but often significant, items, and with these I correlated what I had previously gathered from the ancient chronicles and records, as well as the later books, pamphlets and comments. As a result, I found that answers to some of the problems came into my mind. This book is the result.

I believed, in short, that the reader would enjoy the close, logical reasoning of crime stories as applied to the unravelling of the threads of historical mystery, and to the portrayal of a medieval rebel's character. While not the first to write about Jack Cade, I am, I believe, the first to explain in a reasoned manner some of the more difficult points of his career, and also the first, I hope, to do belated justice to the imaginative possibilities of the story, and to have used my feet as well as my head in a kind of peripatetic research.

I have set out not to tell scholars what they know already or to parade a sterile erudition, but to give life to what has so often consisted of a bald recital of facts and dates. Wherever possible I have, without departing from the truth, employed a modicum of the technique of the writer of detective fiction to give colour and impart excitement to the narrative. Perhaps history should not be written with imagination. Perhaps it should always be dull, as are many of the books my conscience compelled me to read before I felt competent to write this account. Only the reader can decide, and he is my primary concern.

Because this tale is meant to be read with enjoyment rather than as a quarry for facts and data (though it contains many), I have omitted all distracting and irritating reference numerals and footnotes in tiny print. Those items the reader should study for himself are reproduced as Appendices.

Wherever the facts admit of various interpretations I give the alternatives, while making no secret of my own preference. I do not seek to bludgeon the reader into agreeing with me. I have also tried to allow for the differences in outlook between the man of the fifteenth century and ourselves; but I do not believe that in essence men's motives and thinking have so greatly changed in 500 years as to be incomprehensible. If this were so, Shakespeare himself would lie unread and unacted.

The reader will accept my word that I have used and read all the works cited in the bibliography. Nothing is easier than to compile a bibliography listing only what should have been read, but wasn't. Mine is not of this type, but does not include many other books, read *in toto* or of which the relevant pages have been consulted, because these tell nothing new.

The staff of the Reference Library of the Eastbourne Public Library have borrowed for me many rare and indispensable volumes, and have aided me greatly in tracing obscure references and data. To them I am most grateful. I am indebted also to the City Libraries of Sheffield and Manchester and to various County Libraries for the facilities offered, and for their expert advice. Friendly librarians at the smaller libraries of towns such as Ashford, Dartford, Rochester, and other points on the Cade map, may have wondered why a stranger should ask curious questions and rummage feverishly among their stock. Now, they will know.

At one time it seemed possible that Lord Avon (Sir Anthony Eden he then was) might justly claim descent from Alexander Iden, the Sheriff of Kent mentioned in these pages. I have to thank him for his courteous provision of information to assist me in investigating this. Unfortunately, research in this direction was inconclusive. Lord Avon's family originated in the north of England, and I could not trace any connection with the Idens of Kent.

Mr Claud Blair of the Arms and Armour Society kindly gave me much useful information to aid my search for facts regarding the weapons and armour of the fifteenth century, for which I now thank him. I also owe a debt to the Guildhall Library for the loan of certain illustrations.

Lastly, I owe gratitude to my wife, who, as always, encouraged me in my work, and has read with her customary care through the proofs.

As an appendix I have included some notes on Wat Tyler because they bear on the story of Cade. Much more is known of Tyler, and in all respects his character is less complex, his rebellion – if it can in any sense be called his – more straightforward. However, it serves to enrich and amplify the more subtle insurrection of the Captain of Kent. Here I have relied for the most part on the Chronicles and Froissart, and on the excellent and straightforward accounts by Oman. Some of the peregrinations of Tyler and his men correspond to those of the men of 1450, but I do not claim to have covered on foot all the course they ran. Nor do I claim to have introduced any novel discoveries or interpretations.

There is much in the story of the Peasant Revolt of 1381 of interest, and, indeed, my pleasure in writing it was little less than that of writing the first account; but the pleasure was of a different quality. It was like writing a straightforward adventure yarn after having laboured for years on a psychological novel. There was a difference, too, in the background to their compilation. Cade was largely written during a voyage across the Indian Ocean and up to Communist China. Tyler was written in the more prosaic surroundings of my own Sussex village home.

ERIC N. SIMONS

Westham, Sussex, 1961.

ONE

Kent in Arms

[1]

IN MAY of the year 1450 the little town of Ashford in Kent, on the border of the Kentish Weald, lay sheltered by the smooth folds of the Downs. The River Stour, wider and shallower then than now and as yet unbridged, was crossed by a ford at the foot of a dip. This ford, once used by pilgrims on their way to and from the great cathedral at Canterbury, and now known as East Hill, cost twopence to cross, and from it the main street ran up to New Rents. The pinnacled tower of the church gave the town standing and dignity, while the oast-house in the centre spoke of daily human labour.

The road to Ashford was little more than a cart-track, often deeply pitted where men had cut out enough clay to repair their homes and out-houses, as was the custom. Nearer the town, however, it had a firmer surface of gravel and cobbles.

Around the huddle of stout timbered houses and wattle huts that constituted the town, the pasture meadows were lush with grass. Buttercups and dandelions shining in the fitful sunlight scattered their gold lavishly, like improvident heirs. Willows fringed the gentle river, and the fields beyond were green with growing corn and crops, first planted by Caesar's legionaries after they had settled in the fertile acres of the Weald. The predominant impression now was of peace, calm, and simple husbandry. It was a superficial impression.

Placidity of landscape concealed ferment of humanity, a yeasty stirring of passions and resentments. For months wanderers tramping the narrow, uneven, treacherous country lanes had told their woes to all who would listen, made gloomy prophecies, so that after they had gone, they left behind a slowly-spreading stain of shame and resentment. In the April of that same year John Dalby of Brockhampton and London had foretold the coming of 'a marvellous and terrible man of high birth', who, after a battle at Hounslow Heath, would send the King flying and take his crown.

The area pullulated with informers, and for this bold statement he was indicted and punished. Thomas Cheyney, a fuller of Canterbury, known as 'Bluebeard' and pretending to be a hermit, had been executed as an agitator. By now, therefore, men had learned to be discreet. Dangerous truths slid out of the corners of mouths; behind shielding hands; in mutters and whispers. Statements of fact atrophied into hints and sardonic quips, sharp significant glances, a curl of the upper lip at mention of a hated name.

Ashford was a gathering place of farmers, esquires, merchants, traders, maltsters, churchmen, intriguers with their ears to the ground. During the early months of that year, the taverns had been the natural meeting-places of honest souls appalled by the unchastised almost contemptuous raids of the French on Winchelsea and Rye, on the Thames harbours and the ports of East Kent. There, too, came together patriots indignant at the loss of Normandy and the cruel waste of good English blood and treasure on the battlefields of France. In quiet back rooms away from the rough, brawling commonalty grave men spoke, shrewd heads nodded, needy malcontents, touts and Yorkist plotters said their pieces, and discontent like a boil swelled and came to a head. The belief that something would have to be done and done quickly was generated and sustained.

The difficulty was to find a leader untainted by local feud or rivalry, jealousy and suspicion; a leader with a voice that could make itself heard above the petty clamour like a silver trumpet, to serve as symbol and rallying point for men with anger in their hearts and an ache for justice. He must have 'panache' allied to military skill; education; a presence commanding collective respect; authority deriving from birth and breeding; and the courage to risk his head. Above all, he must have the ability to weld into an effective army men dissimilar for the most part in personal standing and objectives, with characters and resources as varied as their occupations – learned men, ignorant men, rich men, poor men, knight and commoner, priest and trader, farmer and fisherman, each and all shot with pride of craft and love of their land.

These secret meetings, these solemn discussions behind closed doors, had hitherto broken down whenever action was proposed because there was among them none big enough, none who combined these essential attributes. Then the miracle happened. To these gloomy, earnest, essentially provincial men there came, one unknown day, the leader they had been seeking, of military experience, from foreign territory, with a persuasive eloquence, proven courage, and a power of decision that could be detected even if, at the outset, it was not manifested. To this day we do not know whence he came; whether he had been invited to join a conspiracy already in being or merely recognised for what he was, a forceful personality, a born commander. He may have ridden into Kent on his way home from Ireland, aflame with ambition, an adventurer lusting for power, a known bastard eager to redeem this humiliation by using for his own ends the turbulence and unrest he had perceived as he travelled across Britain. He may have been thrust up as their elected 'Captain' by the common men of Kent, who knew and trusted him and would follow no other. He may have been the tool of unscrupulous politicians lurking in the dark shadows of that blind alley known as treason, or merely a catalyst turning discontent and rage into an upsurge of will and decision. He is, was, and for ever will be, a man of mystery, product of a brutal and tumultuous age, his entire career a blend of perplexing contradictions, unexplained hesitations, missed opportunities, brilliant tactical victories, and great betrayals. All we have by which to judge him is a handful of old chronicles that have come down to us and the embellishments and distortions of hostile writers eager to toady to a vindictive Court.

The pages that follow tell his story as one man sees it.

[2]

FROM THE little port of Howth, near Dublin, by sea to North Wales, a disembarkation at Beaumaris, thence by road to Chester and beyond, was in the early fifteenth century the favoured route for armies and their generals returning from Ireland. It was the route that had been taken in the reverse direction in 1449 by Richard Duke of York and his wife, Cicely Neville, when they were ordered to that unhappy country. It may be assumed, not unreasonably, that if Cade had been, as is often suggested, a member of the Duke's household, he would have returned by the same route.

The man now known as 'Jack Cade' called himself John Mortimer, and claimed to be a cousin of the Duke of York. Certainly, the Yorkists from the beginning treated his cause as their own. He was sometimes known as 'John Amend-all' because, it was said, he promised to put right all the ills of his day. Shakespeare, whose account of him is biassed and untrue, however inevitable in view of the age in which it was written, makes York say, in *Henry VI*, 'I have seduced a headstrong Kentishman, John Cade, of Ashford, to make commotion as full well he can under the title of John Mortimer . . . For that John Mortimer, which now is dead, in face, in gait, in speech, he doth resemble.'

Shakespeare was writing at a time when glorification of a rebel could hardly have been expected to appeal to Queen

Elizabeth, and might have brought him into danger. He was no historian, and relied too greatly on Hall and Holinshed, now known to be untrustworthy. He accepted, therefore, the lowly origins of the 'Captain of Kent' as fact, and depicted him as a vulgar rabble-rouser, known by his men to be an impostor and no better than themselves.

There was put about after Cade's death a Court theory that as a young man Cade belonged to the household of Sir Thomas Dacre of Sussex, and having murdered a young maidservant when she revealed her pregnancy by him, fled the country. After serving as a common soldier in the French wars – it was hinted that he even fought against his own countrymen – he returned to Kent under the assumed name of 'Dr Aylmer' or 'Aylemere', feigning to be a physician. Here he married the daughter of a squire from Taundede (?Tandredge) in Surrey. This story is unsupported by evidence, and it appears that the Aylmer it mentions was in all probability a John Aylmer of Cade Street in Sussex.

This is but one of the political slanders put about by prejudiced Lancastrian historians in later years. The uncertainty even they felt about his birth and standing is shown by the variety of their statements. Thus, one refers to him as 'the tanner of Ashford'. Shakespeare, in the play abovementioned, makes Bevis call him 'Jack Cade the clothier', but lets Cade say of himself: 'My father was a Mortimer, my mother a Plantagenet, my wife descended of the Lacies. Therefore am I of an honourable house.' Edmund Mortimer, Earl of March, Cade claims in the play, married the daughter of the Duke of Clarence, and by her had twin sons. The elder, being put to nurse, was stolen by a beggarwoman, who, when he became of age, made him a bricklayer. This bricklayer was Cade's father.

We can approximate to the truth about this strange man only by setting down what such evidence as we have suggests is reasonably true. In the first place, if Cade were deliberately chosen to lead the revolt that bears his name, it must have been – could only have been – because he was known to possess military experience, later to be demonstrated in the field. There is some foundation for the belief that he was indeed illegitimate, but the son of Roger Mortimer. As suggested, he may have been a member of the household of the Duke of York in Ireland, and many of his medieval biographers refer to him as an 'Irishman'. It is known that there were illegitimate members of the house of March, and it has always been a common practice for the aristocratic begetters of bastards to find jobs for their progeny about the court or in the households of their families.

Cade almost certainly learned military organisation and tactics as a soldier in France, and possibly perfected his knowledge in Ireland. His sojourn in these two countries combined with his aristocratic connections would give him an accent both superior to and different from that of Kent, which would be an asset in managing less-travelled men. His real or pretended lineage would give him the bearing and dignity of carriage a leader requires, without which the proud gentry of the country, the ecclesiastics and yeomen, would never have placed themselved under his command.

Had he been tanner, clothier, quack, doctor, common soldier, fugitive lackey, bricklayer, he could never have welded headstrong, ill-assorted units into a fanatically loyal and courageous army. Rightly or wrongly, both his followers and the Court believed his claim that good blood ran in his veins. He may not have been 'John Mortimer'. We have no certainty that he was. But everyone, even his adversaries, thought he was at the time, and this is what matters. No contemporary denied his claim or called him a liar until he was a broken and defeated man flying for his life. Then, every attempt was made to discredit and revile the man who had made the royal throne totter.

There is, however, a bare possibility that he was himself a southern Squire or yeoman, because Cade was a not unfamiliar name in parts of Surrey and Sussex. Cades were landed proprietors in the Reigate area up to the seventeenth century.

Perhaps we can sum up this argument best by recording the words of Lord Sackville, written at a much later date: 'Whatever he was by birth, I warrant him a gentleman by his learning.'

According to the chronicles written during or shortly after his period Cade was a young man (said to have been born between 1420 and 1430) 'of goodly stature and right pregnant wit', who went about gaily clad in scarlet. In conference even his adversaries found him 'discreet', while the form and substance of the proclamations he issued show him to have possessed education and verbal skill, even if these may have been first drawn up for him by the literate men of his party. He was familiar with the grievances and feelings of his followers and the nation, and is believed to have been sympathetic to the Yorkist cause; not unlikely if he had, in fact, been a member of the Duke of York's household.

However this may be, his military capacity enabled him to manoeuvre his levies in a manner and with a discipline no illiterate lout could have achieved, certainly not Wat Tyler. He had great energy and persuasiveness, and one chronicle describes him as 'witty in his talkynge and request'.

This, then, was the 'Captain of Kent', the title he chose or was awarded. Between the 24th and 30th May, when the religious festival of Whitsuntide was being celebrated, he and his lieutenants in Kent and, later, Sussex, called up and secretly assembled both the disaffected and the blindly obedient. It is known from existing records that the rebel army was made up of a handful of knights, rather more esquires, a considerable number of 'gentlemen' and yeomen, together with a miscellany of merchants, craftsmen, husbandmen, mariners and constables, besides a mayor or two, a few priests and clerks, and a multitude of the common hewers of wood and drawers of water. (The 'constables' were not police, but constables (state officers) of 'hundreds', a hundred being one of the areas into which in medieval times the counties were divided, each hundred having its own court.)

The hundreds of Kent included Bleangate, Westgate, Downhamford, Kinghamford, Twyford, Ashort, Dartford, Tunbridge, Alvesbridge, Ringslow, Hadlow, Calehill, Barnfield, Larkfield, Littlefield, Washingstone, Stouthing, Tolingtrough, Ospring and Shamwell, all of which had importance.

The ordinary folk of the county were all officially called up with the proper form and ceremony by the authorities they knew to be lawful. (The constables of no fewer than thirty-three hundreds despatched the writs.) From seven mainly Wealden villages every man capable of bearing arms was taken. Slowly, on foot, on horseback, in carts and wagons, the insurgents trickled towards their appointed place of assembly, somewhere in the centre of Kent. There they were drilled, marched, fed, and given arms, equipment and orders. They saw and heard the great John Mortimer himself, were harangued by, acclaimed and applauded, him, recognised his stature and superiority, became eager to follow wherever he led.

[3]

A TRAVELLER arriving in England in 1449 would, had he ridden westwards along the Sussex coast, have rapidly detected one of the sources of the anger and dismay he had encountered ever since he crossed the border of that county. Gazing first out to sea and speculating on the hidden location of Winchelsea, an old town buried long before by the waters, he would have observed the walls of the new town, which had replaced the original, cresting the spur of the Downs. He would have ridden into the town itself, perhaps, and smelt the sour smell of recently-extinguished burning, seen the breached walls, witnessed the still unrepaired damage and destruction wrought by the French. There had been more than one attack, so that now, her harbour silting up, her inhabitants ragged folk picking a living among the ruins, the hitherto prosperous port was dying fast, if not already dead.

Even busy, flourishing Rye (closer to the sea and now, with the decline of Winchelsea, one of the main ports of the south, nicely placed on a hill above Romney marsh) was a sorry litter of blackened timbers, collapsed mud-and-wattle, shattered walls, and dejected, bewildered townsmen slowly picking up the threads of a disrupted existence, their eyes constantly on the sea beyond the harbour, for fear of being taken unawares by the sails of the hated French bearing down upon them again.

These raids, however distressing, were but a local humiliation, one only among the many causes that were to send simple, honest men storming furiously to London. There were more important grievances. The French raids were embittering and resented, certainly, but in addition there was the savage enmity between Yorkist and Lancastrian eddying darkly in country brains. The clever, cunning Yorkist politicians were ever on the scene when unrest appeared, to begin – like the modern Communists – a hungry angling in troubled waters, not always without success.

No revolution occurs without cause. Agitator, politician, malcontent, power-seeker, can achieve nothing that will make men ready to shed each other's blood unless there is a sore in hearts and minds that stridency pricks. Cade's revolt was no exception. The old chronicles are inclined to rest content with the simple statement that 'the Commons of Kent rose' under their great Captain. By 'Commons' they did not mean only the humble, unlettered, poor whom Shakespeare portrays as Cade's principal followers. They meant the slowly-emerging provincial middle-class, and recognised in the rising the protest of worthy members of this class against undeniable injustice and oppression. There were many decent comfortable folk unencumbered by self-seeking in the rebel army. Many of the poorer class were there as well, but most of these were equally inspired by more than a yearning for loot. They were ordinary men doing what they knew and felt to be their duty.

This was, indeed, one of those recurring periods in English history when a weak, irresolute government is everywhere despised and abominated; when it lies supine before foreign insolence; when its rich, ambitious men are more concerned with their personal prestige and the stimulating game of acquisition and power than with such immaterial matters as honour, justice and pity. It was a period in some ways strangely reminiscent of the bitter years before 1939. Many voices were to be heard crying out for a 'leader' who should cut away the rotten growths of greed and cruelty about the throne, restore their pride, bring back prosperity to the humble. Political dissension – again as in 1939 – was a network of cancer running right through the land. So, when the men of Kent drew the sword it was as if a tremor shook the south. Spontaneously, there were risings in East Sussex and even as far afield as Suffolk and Essex. Contingents from these counties were soon marching down leafy lanes or alongside reedy pools and fens to join the rebel Captain.

Nevertheless, the rising was essentially Kentish in origin. It was born in Kentish hearts and heads, supported by Kentish self-interest, stimulated by Kentish money, encouraged and spiritually guided by Kentish clerics. Any benefits that might accrue to England as a nation were merely incidental to the main objective, which was primarily – at all events in the intention of the leaders – to break the ring of greedy nobles about King Henry VI, and make their way through to present to him in person their legitimate complaints. This does not mean that the rebels were all small-minded and unpatriotic; but to them their own county came first. If they thought about it at all, they assumed that there could not be a decent, prosperous England without a decent, prosperous Kent.

Kent was, in fact, in that period one of the most enlightened of all the English counties. She exported large quantities of wool, cloth, wine and miscellaneous items to the continent of Europe, and was therefore quickly affected by wars and by the blunders of administrators and politicians. The incursion of traders from other lands had quickened the local intelligence. The merchants of the county provided useful foreign news to the Court and its hangers-on. Moreover, the living conditions of Kentish men and women had steadily improved over the decades. Anything that weakened Kent could, therefore, be regarded as weakening England. There was some justification for the parochialism of the squires, traders and farmers who made up the bulk of Cade's band.

During the past few years, however, a depression had set in, so that over a period of two years the export of cloth had fallen by 35 per cent, of wine by 50 per cent, and of other items by 23 per cent. This not only reduced incomes, till in some places no one was earning as much as £100 a year; it also reduced the amount of money available for public works. It was for this reason that the harbours of the Cinque Ports were silting up, and as a result, the bigger ships with their valuable loads were having to be diverted to rival ports. As we have seen, foreign pirates roamed unchallenged in the Channel, but the naval convoys that should have protected English shipping from them could not readily find harbour owing to this silting in Kentish ports. Flanders, Holland, Zeeland, had banned the importation of English cloth, and throughout the county the profitable trade in wax, hides and cloth had declined. Taxes were direct, heavy and hotly resented.

Then there was the Statute of Labourers. This Statute regulated the relations between landowners and their peasantry, and had been rendered obnoxious by unscrupulous tinkering at its provisions, to the detriment of freeholders. The wages of the peasantry had fallen till they had barely enough to eat. The weakness of the Government could be perceived in the growing number of rapes, robberies, murders and deliberate arsons. The malefactors responsible were either not caught, or if brought to trial, often protected by those whose minions they were. The feeble King was known to be at the mercy of his rapacious and quarrelsome nobles, while his French consort surrounded herself with a bevy of parasites costing money that Henry's finances could not easily supply, and that was in any event more than the country could afford.

Over and above all this, corruption, muddle and greed ran through the administration from the King's ministers downwards. The King and his household could insist by law on being provisioned and housed whenever they chose to move from London, but instead of offering fair prices for what they received, they compelled those who supplied their necessities to accept payment at ridiculous rates, payment not in good hard cash, but in drafts on the Treasury which were not only dishonourably ignored on many occasions, but also were sometimes issued without authority by underlings for their own benefit.

The ruinous cost of the wars with France was another sore point. These squabbles had rendered the King virtually bankrupt and brought penury to many of his subjects, yet the waste and luxury of his household, the extravagance of his wife and her court, the rapacity of his nobles, were unaffected, and, what is more, obvious to even the poorest countryman. Even the King's justice was sold without shame to the highest bidder by ministers, sheriffs, members of the Privy Council, bailiffs and the rest. You got only what you paid for. There was no such thing as 'right'.

Unjust taxation was but one of the lashes that flicked and stung. Men who had no interest whatsoever in hunting were compelled to pay the hunting tax, and it was arranged with diabolical cunning that any defaulter could be summoned to court and fined for non-payment even before proper notice had been given. Consequently the man concerned could often not reach the court that was to try him in time to defend himself. (It took some defaulters as much as five days to get to Canterbury, for example, from the remote parts of the county where they had their homes.) The writs by which such offenders were summoned were known as 'The writs of the green wax'. Soon there was not a man in Kent who did not fear for his farm, his home, his humble possessions. Many weavers, fullers, dyers, women carders, combers, spinners, buyers and sellers of cloth, were unemployed – and there was then no 'dole'.

Even the gentry of the county were themselves, in fact, at the mercy of the nobles. They could vote only if they had freehold land or property of forty shillings in value. Many freemen had no vote, unless they were prepared under pressure to vote as their rulers desired. To recoup themselves for the money extorted from them in taxes, merchants and traders were compelled to put up their prices. There was therefore a flourishing 'black market' in artificially scarce commodities, and those who ran it waxed fat on the proceeds, even buying their way into county families, some of which endure to this day, and probably take pains to conceal that they are descended from the black-marketeers of the past . . .

It cannot be too strongly emphasised that Kent had been until then a well-ordered county, the inhabitants of which had a sturdy independence. Even her landlords had had no special rights. On the whole the labourer had been well paid and well treated. It was the threatened break-up of this advanced social community and its 'way of life' that incensed the gentry, squires and commons of West Kent. Control of the English Channel had been torn from them. Now and again freebooters in the 'commando' tradition went off to sea on their own and captured a few French vessels. But what happened? They were not allowed to keep their booty. It was taken away from them and not even distributed as compensation among those who had suffered most from the depredations of the French pirate ships. Instead, it was sold to line the pockets of Lord Saye, of whom more shall be heard in due course. Moreover, the very merchants whose warehouses in the ports had been looted and burned, and whose trade had been badly hit by the reluctance of foreigners to send their vessels to England, had their stocks of merchandise in France seized in revenge, while the ships they ventured to send abroad were never safe.

Thus, the Cade rebellion was not, in its inception, a disloyal act, but an outburst of popular indignation, with legitimate and clearly stated aims, which shall presently be detailed. Not once did it threaten or promise to remove the King from his throne and substitute for him either usurper, demagogue or soldier. The declared objective was the defence of the Crown against the lords, and the bringing into existence of a new government, strong enough to defend and protect the country and her interests, to restore prosperity to Kent; in short, to get the rich off the backs of the poor.

TWO

Blackheath

[1]

THE SECRECY with which the rebel forces had assembled was
matched by that with which they marched to their destination,
a patch of open plain between Eltham and Greenwich –
Blackheath – already notorious as the place where an earlier
rebel from Kent, Wat Tyler, had once pitched camp, and
where the stentorian voice of the English revolutionary, John
Ball, had sounded in the ears of an assembled multitude.
Today, grassy, respectable, its green stretches traversed by
well-kept paths, encompassed by a mass of houses, schools
and civic buildings, of shops, restaurants and garages, it has
no rebellions, no suggestion of violence and combat. Not even
the Communists use it for their meetings, nor do energetic
peace-lovers squat down upon its turf. As for London, there
is no need to march. Ample wheeled transport of one sort or
another can be used to take whoever wills to the metropolis.

Nevertheless, even now its suitability for military use is
plain, and indeed it was a camp for the training of recruits in
World War I and World War II. There is, however, one
survival that has interest. Away to the right is a wood,
vestigial remains of a thick forest. It is possible that through
this Cade's army marched.

The number of that army has been the subject of much
conjecture, and the figure suggested ranges from a few

thousand to over forty thousand. For logistic reasons this last figure can be dismissed. Not even a military genius could have secretly fed, equipped and efficiently manoeuvred so large a number of men in the wastes of medieval England for any length of time. The roads, though better than they were to become later in the century, were miry, waterlogged after rain, and treacherous. Not only this, but little heed was paid to their maintenance, not because their importance had diminished or their necessity was not appreciated, but because no organisation existed for their regular upkeep. The public spirit of rich men now and again provided the funds for this work, but at numerous points the few bridges were shaky or completely down. The sappers of Cade's force had themselves to bridge whatever streams they encountered before they could be crossed by the main body, unless a suitable ford could be discovered.

As they drew nearer to their destination, the soldiers found their progress hampered by roads as crowded with traffic and almost as congested as our own, though their capacity was far more limited. The merchants bringing goods from the ports and their warehouses were liable at any time to be attacked by robbers, mounted or on foot, to minimise this risk they travelled on horseback in large convoys, taking much of the available space. The rest was filled intermittently by hucksters, pedlars, chapmen, clerks, tinkers, beggars, wandering preachers, and journeymen dodging the Statute of Labourers and slyly slipping into another county to find work. All these encumbered the roads, while in addition a few high-ranking personages travelled down the highway with scores of followers trailing after them.

Some of these itinerants were doubtless swept into Cade's levies as they dribbled along the foot-tracks, lanes and arteries of Kent, but as no means then existed whereby news of the rising could be instantaneously circulated and the ways be held open for the marching men, many innocent unsuspecting travellers coming to the south-east from London must have been surprised, thrust aside or compelled to force a way past the troops whose progress delayed and impeded them.

Much of the county was then uncultivated, and everywhere were forests, heath and marshland. Around the villages were only a few clearings, split into long narrow strips for the growing of produce. All the conveniently near good land surrounding these clearings was devoted to pasturage. The few scattered towns were walled, and their gateways barred at night, so that in themselves these constituted a series of bottle-necks through which the army had to pass.

The concensus of opinion is that Cade never mustered more than twenty thousand men, but even this figure seems too high, because when he later received news that the King had assembled an army of around this number to oppose him, he carefully avoided contact with it. The more likely figure for his force is between ten and fifteen thousand. Had his army been equal in numbers to that of the King he would probably have stood his ground and given battle. It is unusual for a superior force to surrender an advantageous position without a struggle.

Assuming this estimate to be correct, then the astonishing speed with which the rebels arrived and assembled at Black-heath can be more easily appreciated. Their very speed, however, obscures the means by which they travelled, but there is the authority of local tradition for assuming that a small, compact, well-organised force was joined by other similar bodies at the appointed places of assembly, then marched along the one adequate trunk road, the Roman highway of Watling Street, towards the Heath. As they went, first one small detachment, then another and another, came trickling in from this district and that – East Kent, West Kent, Surrey – along the route.

The fields Cade's men saw being turned over by primitive ploughs drawn by oxen, were unenclosed. Here and there they passed recently-built churches and other ecclesiastical edifices, while some of the older churches had been enlarged.

Their complicated and extravagant architecture would be as exciting and startling to the less sophisticated rustic soldiers as the skyline of New York was to those of our own day.

At halts, chatting with curious wayfarers, pilgrims, friars, the servants of the manor houses going on their errands, the marching men would gather news of this local misdeed and the other committed by those against whom they were marching; but more significant of the condition of England than these anecdotes and complaints would be the intangible, invisible, ever-present atmosphere of terror.

Although they had ceased to be serfs, the honest men ploughing their strips, chaffering in markets, drinking their ale at taverns, were afraid. They never knew whether the drinker in the hostelry was tale-bearer or true man. They never knew when someone might knock on their doors with demands which, if refused, would mean eventually an unfair trial with no redress. They poured out to these momentarily resting soldiers, known to be trudging towards London on their behalf, all the bitterness and anger of their days; but their voices, their faces, the very words they used, betrayed their fear. Rough peasant, infantryman, bearded mariner, bluff and hearty squire, esquire and trader, were confirmed and strengthened by these men they met in their determination to set things right.

It is not improbable that Cade's army was reinforced by more than one such casually-met traveller, all the more because it was plain to those who watched and considered that their ranks were well-disciplined and orderly.

[2]

SWINGING AND SINGING down the winding ways went men from Shepway and Scray, Aylesford and Sutton-at-Hone, Eastry, Petham, Preston, Wingham. The Isle of Thanet had sent its contingents, too. Nevertheless, the bulk of the force came from Ashford, Canterbury, Chatham, Rochester and Maidstone. There exists a satirical dirge to the tune of which they marched (see Appendix I). It ridicules the hated potentates of the time, those false priests and avaricious or incompetent ministers against whom the rising was directed – the Duke of Suffolk (executed the previous year at sea), the Bishop of Hereford, the Bishop of Chester, the Bishop of Salisbury (assassinated shortly after the death of Suffolk), the Abbot of Gloucester, the Bishop of Rochester, the Provost of Eton, the Bishop of Worcester, Cardinal Kempe, and Lord Saye (or Say), great figures in the tragic events that followed. Many other names also appear in these mocking lines.

We may imagine that as the band tramped on, picked and eloquent soldiers (*voces clamantes*) were sent ahead of the main body with a roving commission to scour the roads, give news of the rising, enlist or coerce all who welcomed or sympathised with the rebel cause. These showy, virile figures would ride up to the timbered houses of the farmers, the peasant huts, the manor houses and taverns, the bow-and-arrow shooting galleries, the halls surrounding the gate-houses, and speak their piece. They would stop to exhort the drivers of the newish two-wheeled carts with their spike iron wheels, these drivers bestriding the horse and not the cart. Almost certainly, as is the way of soldiers, they would 'knock off', 'win', 'snaffle', a clutch of eggs, the odd fowl, even a sheep or two or a fat, untended porker, for sustenance, living off the country as they went. It is because of these tricks that there was put about in later decades the statement, often repeated, that Cade's men 'pillaged the country'.

One sees them like colourful romantic players announcing the forthcoming arrival of a circus as they moved through the gaping huddles of wandering folk. The humble worshippers on their way to shrines and praying-points; the maimed and stumping soldiery back from France, begging for alms as they made their way to London or their native villages; the rogues, the vagabonds, the suspected witches; the loose

C

women, apprentices, pedlars from foreign parts, all turned curious, hopeful or wary eyes on these advance guards. As night fell, the reconnoitring soldiers would seek out the nearest inn to buy themselves a skewer full of bacon, a flagon of ale, some cheeses and pickles, whatever the houses had to offer, or were under compulsion to offer for fear of bringing down wrath upon their hosts' heads. It may well be that on occasion the innkeepers had to whistle for their money, but more probably they received their due. Their guests were recruiting-sergeants as well as serving soldiers. If a dispute arose, it was in all likelihood because of overcharge or inferior food.

In these inns they would doubtless bargain for the provisioning of the army behind them. Cade had money – much of it from secret supporters among the wealthier merchants of London – and there is no record to suggest that what was ultimately received in the way of food and drink or whatever was needed was not honourably paid for. The tale of pillage is a slander.

The few imaginative novelists who have dealt with this period have erroneously depicted the army that marched on Blackheath as a rabble equipped with nothing but the primitive weapons of peasants – scythes, billhooks, truncheons, pitchforks and staves. It would be foolish to deny that among the more hastily recruited rustics such instruments of war were visible, but the core of the force was trained, well-drilled, and far better equipped than this would suggest. (Trained regular soldiers have rarely been defeated in a pitched battle by the rough-and-ready weapons of a mob.) It is abundantly clear that the King's Court would never have panicked before a loose and irregular collection of novices. The revolution of 1381 had taught them better. It was the news and the proof that *an army of formidable character and equipment* was marching on London that terrified them. They had enough spies at work to know the truth about the insurgents' strength.

However this may be, on to the plains of Blackheath, where one hundred and fifty-odd years later, King James and his Scots were to bring the game of golf to England, thousands of armed soldiers came pouring, and proceeded with skill and celerity to throw up what even the chroniclers of the time recognised as a 'camp'. This camp was as efficiently constructed and devised as if it had been built in France during the disastrous wars of the reign, which is not so remarkable as it may sound. A camp is not the same as a bivouac or billets. It is a position enabling the armed men of a temporarily stationary force to eat and sleep in the open (as distinct from in towns or villages), so that not only are they immediately ready for assembly when action is imminent, but also they can be more easily subjected to discipline; and it must be recalled that the discipline of English fighting men was, even in those times, one of their great superiorities over the French soldiery.

While the men at arms probably slept in tents, a palisade surrounding the camp would need to be built, and communal erections for the usual military and domestic purposes constructed. Cade's followers included thatchers, sawyers, joiners and wood turners, craftsmen of energy and knowledge. They included butchers and bakers; spicers to deal with prepared food; smiths, lead-workers, braziers and cutlers to repair and fashion arms; saddlers and farriers, grooms and drovers, to care for horses, cattle and transport vehicles; scriveners and clerks to perform the necessary clerical work; and trumpeters to sound the calls. Hardly a craft or trade of the period, hardly an occupation but was represented.

The camp these men would have to build would be made up of a collection of buildings placed as far as possible on high ground commanding the roads by way of which it might be attacked. It would occupy, therefore, a good defensive position. Possibly the Cator Estate, Blackheath Park, Morden Road and Morden College stand on the very site of the ditches and stakes of Jack Cade's resting-place.

There would be a portcullis consisting of logs, roughly hewn, and a gate at which sentries were posted. Behind the protective palisades would be the camp kitchens, the baggage wagons and the wooden shooting-barriers or shields. There may even have been stalls and booths where the soldiers could obtain amusement and entertainment of the kinds they preferred. Armed men guarded the perimeter, and wherever open spaces had been provided there was drilling, and practice-shooting with the crossbow from behind a shield. Ever and again the trumpet calls of the time sounded, food was cooked, men ate and drank. Ditches were dug around the entire camp, as a safeguard against attack.

One cannot but regret that apart from a few helmets in churches, no British armour made or used before the sixteenth century is known, so that our notions of what arms and armour were used by Cade can be derived only from illustrations in illuminated manuscripts and effigies on monuments.

The archers wore jacks or sleeveless tunics of simple form, and steel caps, extremely varied in design. The armour worn by the knights and esquires had by 1450 become less elaborate than in the preceding decades, but was much more colourful, as will be seen. Breast- and back-plates were covered by vivid short coats over chain mail, which was sewn on to a doublet of fustian. Instead of these pieces of chain-mail the practice had recently come in of wearing expensive cloaks ornamented with fur. Sometimes the plates of steel armour were concealed by rich velvets covering the body and studded with gold.

[3]

THE MORE CLOSELY one studies the actions of 'The Captain of Kent', the more one is brought hard up against one's own incomprehensions. It is this that makes the man so mysterious. It is clearly recorded that he and his troops remained for a full seven days in the camp at Blackheath, idle on the great common, high up above London, and apparently drawing no nearer at all to the great objective with which they had come out of the by-ways of Kent and tramped the hard Roman road of Watling Street.

It is extraordinary that a rebel army essaying to march on the capital city for the sole purpose, it had been announced, of liberating the King and dealing with his ministers, should loiter and delay. There is sufficient of the military Hamlet about Cade to make him a fascinating figure for the impartial student. If his original plan was to camp at Blackheath, hoping to terrify the royal forces by his very presence, it was a sad miscalculation, and in any event belies the military ability of the man. But if this was not the plan, what purpose was served by wasting the élan of an enthusiastic army? For what reason had its assembly been so secret, its march so rapid, if in the end it was designed to be kept hanging about for seven whole days doing nothing?

An insurrection once launched must be kept going, must reap the tactical advantage of surprise, strike before the opposing loyal forces have had time to deploy.

There are a number of possible explanations of this unwise halt. Two of them, at least, are logical, if unlikely. The first is that Cade, though brilliant in the field, was subject to moments of indecision; unable, like Hitler in World War II, to make up his mind which of two alternatives to adopt until some 'inner voice' had spoken. This possibility can be entertained for one reason only, namely, that at a later date in his career, a similar, apparently inexplicable halt took place in Cade's military progress.

The alternative explanation, made by some historians, is that Cade displayed his forces for so long at Blackheath for the express purpose of luring the royal army into fighting him on his own chosen ground deep in Kent, every inch of which he knew, and that his conspicuous encampment was a decoy and nothing more. This, however, is hardly a tenable argument, on military grounds alone, and bears the marks of wisdom after the event. The dramatic appearance of expertly led and numerous, armed and disciplined insurgents at the throat of London had, as will be indicated, thrown both the civil and military authorities into confusion and dismay. The Court was away from the capital with all or most of its men, and consequently the capital was at Cade's mercy if he moved in upon it with speed and power. He did not. He loitered for a week.

Other explanations are somewhat more probable. There may have been dissension and doubt in Cade's own camp. His authority was still recent. His skill in war had yet to be put to the test in conflict. No revolutionary leader has been without some men under his command who secretly believe they know better than he, or are jealous of and seek to weaken his authority, lest some day it shall become uncontrollable. Cade may have had to halt to fight his private battle within the tents and win it.

Though a possible explanation, it is not necessarily a true one. There is one still more probable. This is that Cade hoped for a rising simultaneous with his own by his allies in London. Key points of the city would then be in friendly hands, the gates be thrown open, London Bridge be clear for the passage of his army, and he would be able to march in and take over the city without bloodshed, like Wat Tyler.

One conceives him waiting impatiently day after day while messengers bring promises of help, money, tokens of support, but no intimation of active revolt. Meantime, his men circulate in the surrounding countryside, getting in supplies wherever they can be found, and making ready amid long spells of boredom for the grim work they will have to do.

Or possibly supplies had fallen too low by the time he reached Blackheath, and Cade was compelled to pause until his lieutenants and secret allies in the city had brought money and food to meet his needs. Failing success in this, he could not maintain his position, until at last he realised that London

was not going to do his work for him, and that he would have
to wait until he was stronger before marching in.

Finally, there is the most convincing explanation of all,
which is that he needed time to mould the heterogeneous
levies into a tactical weapon. Despite their enthusiasm, their
discipline and courage, these men were not yet an *army*. They
had had little, if any, opportunity up to now to manoeuvre as
a coherent mass. In consequence, if they were to meet professional soldiers, they had to be taught not only to march
and shoot as platoons and companies, but also to move in
great numbers with precision and speed, to take up a proper
order of battle under fire, to deploy, attack, counter-attack,
entrench themselves, understand the signals of command,
wheel and outflank, or if necessary, retreat in good order.

So, perhaps, these seven days were needed to drill and
train them in the fresh invigorating air of the Heath, so that
when the time came, and it was coming soon, they should
hold their own with the experienced royal troops expected to
confront them when they showed themselves in London. But
this would need more than a week, and it is also possible that
heavy rain may have fallen, leaving the Heath a sea of mud,
and hampering concerted movement. So, when it became
known that the King was at last moving out of London to
destroy the rebels with an army, outnumbering their own
and showing none of the expected signs of mutiny, Cade may
have felt that he had no option but to retreat.

The facts are, whatever the explanation, that he halted for
this week at Blackheath, then retreated southwards until he
came to the little town of Sevenoaks (Senocke) in Kent. Since
he could not avoid a battle against odds, it was better to fight
on a more suitable field than the wide, flat expanse of
Blackheath, ideal for the movements of an army trained in
formal warfare. There was a point beyond Sevenoaks where
the configuration of the ground was such that if the King's
men could be drawn forward thus far, they would lie open to
an outflanking movement, cutting them off from their base.

There were also interesting possibilities of ambush, for the one practicable military road ran through wooded country, while at the tiny village of Sole Field or Solefields there was a ravine capable of concealing many warriors. His men were more used to this country than the Londoners.

Thus, while he had of necessity to retreat, he could take advantage of the withdrawal. Cade almost certainly accounted for this backward movement by telling his men that he had in mind the sack of Lord Saye's great house at Knole in Sevenoaks.

The theory that his original advance on Blackheath was a feint is weak precisely because there was no need for Cade to have wasted time, money and supplies in a dash at express speed with his entire force to the great Common. A detachment would have been sufficient if the aim was to lure the King forward. He could have held back his main force as Tyler did and used it to take Knole and the town of Sevenoaks itself, while still having time to form up and meet the royal troops on his chosen ground. He had a good deal of support in the area around Blackheath, and he would have done much better to inspire and keep contact with them, while sending his best troops to take London, than to hide in the woods of Sevenoaks and Solefields in the hope of being followed.

THREE

The Captain Demands

[1]

THE READER must choose for himself from the many explanations of Cade's delay and retreat. Meantime, we shall leave
the insurgents still in camp at Blackheath and turn to London
itself, the prize of victory. In that city none were more
terrified by the news of Cade's rising than the ecclesiastics,
particularly the corrupt and greedy Bishops, whose names,
chanted in ribald fashion, had resounded in the Kentish lanes
to the sound of tramping feet. Instead of standing by the
King, their patron, they fled to their sees and dioceses, which
had seen but little of them during the last few years, fearing
that if Cade should take London they would be put to death,
as the Bishop of Salisbury had been not long before.

It is undeniable that these prelates were associated with
some of the worst deeds and vices of the period, but before
they are too strongly condemned, the conditions under which
they exercised their offices must be recognised. Most of them
came from aristocratic families or had achieved high position
in the castles and courts of influential nobles and princes.
Their education had been thorough and had involved much
sacrifice of leisure and the more exciting pursuits. Many of
them had been sent abroad to study, and at the universities
there had been exposed to all the weakening influences of a
different way of life. They had come back to their native land

not only hard up and even in debt, but with the feeling that
society owed them a great deal for the sacrifices they had
made. Expectation of life was much lower in those days, and
they had to make a lot of money quickly if they were now to
get out of life what they felt they had missed.

Their return had placed them in the unfortunate position
that they could make money quickly only by accepting bribes
from penitents who sought absolution. They were believed
also to foster lawsuits for their own ends. They cared nothing
for public opinion, and did nothing to raise their Church or
themselves in popular esteem. Instead, they quarrelled
furiously with one another, friars attacking Bishops and being
attacked in return. Many scholars and priests protested
against the behaviour of their fellows and the infamy it
heaped upon the Church, and this, doubtless, explains why a
number of abbots and priests were included among the
followers of Cade. The Church as an institution did nothing
to redeem herself. In the hands of privileged leaders, she was
so rich that popular clamour to her meant nothing. She relied
upon the secular arm for her defence, and completely ignored
the unpleasant truth that the minds over which she pre-
dominated were no longer those of totally ignorant churls.
She lived still in the world of Boccaccio, with its revealing
picture of the relations between monks and simple peasants,
before men had learned to think for themselves, and when the
most incredible deceits could be practised by the learned and
unscrupulous upon the trusting and credulous.

The world was changing, however, even in the fifteenth
century, but the ecclesiastics had either not discovered it, or
were determined to arrest the change. The Bishops, had they
and their Pope been willing, could have set in motion reforms
that would have taken much of the fire out of the hearts of
rebellious Englishmen; they did nothing.

It would be wrong, nevertheless, to imagine that they were
essentially vicious. Some were, some were not. The trouble
with them was that they were business managers rather than

spiritual guides. Their job, as they saw it, in the circumstances of the age, was to keep on the right side of the King, who gave them their clerical preferments – with the tacit permission of the Pope of Rome – and then appointed them to high office in the State. Consequently, their function became that of highly-paid bureaucrats. In effect they constituted an embryonic civil service, without its modern traditions and training. In collaboration with the nobles, and sometimes without it, they provided the secretaries, the administrators, the treasurers, the chancellors, the recorders and organisers. Of them all, the subtlest was probably Cardinal Kempe, the Lord Chancellor. At times they constituted a buffer between King Henry and his barons. They worked hard, but it was basically work for the State rather than for their flock.

With so much purely administrative and secular work to do, they could not but be neglectful of their duties to their sees. As a result the slackness and immorality of many Rectors was ignored; the worst papal practices were allowed to be advocated, such as the selling of pardons and indulgences; the urgent needs of the people were left unfulfilled. Yet they were ever swift to do battle for their own privileges and endowments, and had no mercy on heretics and heresy. If the Cade rising did nothing else, it showed plainly their unpopularity and the contempt they had aroused.

[2]

PARLIAMENT was in session at Leicester when a messenger whose name and status are unknown brought to the King's Court the first news of the rising. If their own interests were threatened, the Court could act quickly enough. As was customary, the masters of the country, the great lords, had most of their personal fighting men with them. They resembled, were the progenitors of, the modern gangster with his attendant body of thugs, or the Fascist chiefs with their 'bruisers' ever ready. They had no hesitation in breaking up the proceedings, and scurried back to London with the King, who was virtually their prisoner, to face what even they perceived was a serious threat to their existence.

Between the 7th and 13th June, or in other words during the week wasted by Cade at Blackheath, a royal army of between fifteen and twenty thousand men was got together in the capital, after a march of a hundred miles or so. The King himself was deposited like left-luggage in the Priory of St John at Clerkenwell, while the army itself camped near by at Clerkenwell Fields. (The Priory of St John possessed great wealth and was famous as the seat in England of the Knights Hospitallers of the Order of St John of Jerusalem. It had a noble gateway, which in 1450 had been erected only forty years or so before. It is today the headquarters of the St John Ambulance Association.)

The retainers of the nobles had been reinforced by the levies of London and the Home Counties, quickly called up. The wealthy Aldermen and Councillors of the city experienced vast relief when this strong army, with the King in their midst, made its way through the narrow streets. They were encouraged thereby to exert themselves on their own account and strengthen the defences around London Bridge, over which, if he attacked, Cade must come to London.

There seems to have been almost as much dilatoriness among the royal commanders as in Cade's camp. The bolder tacticians wished to advance at once on Blackheath, and with the aid of their experienced soldiers, whom they took to be invincible when hurled against raw untrained churls, drive Cade from the approaches, and cut him to ribbons as he fled back towards Kent. The more cautious, however, and the more cunning, sought to discover first, by direct inquiry, what the Captain of Kent desired, and what his price might be for abandoning his plan, dispersing his troops, and accepting a pardon for himself. They wanted to know, in short, if he were tractable, could be bribed, or was a genuine fanatic with whom it would be impossible to treat. They sought to save themselves cheaply if they could. One might even call their method 'dollar diplomacy'.

The issue was almost certainly decided at a Council meeting held on 10th June. A picked body of diplomats, representing both the Court and the Church, were then chosen to seek out Cade at his headquarters, and confer with him. While these negotiations were taking place, more time would be gained to put the defences in order and to bring in supplies for the assembled army.

There is no doubt that this meeting with Cade took place, but there is some difference of opinion among the historians regarding the conditions obtaining in his camp on their arrival. One school maintains that there was little discipline and no leadership generally accepted until the King's envoys arrived. In justification they quote the writer who says: 'And as good was Jack Robin as John at the Noke, for all were as high as pig's feet; until the time came when they should come and speak with such states and messengers as were sent unto them. Then they put all their power into the man that was named Captain of all the host.'

Another account, much more trustworthy, says, however, that Thomas Cocke or Cooke, a young draper of London, born in Lavenham, Suffolk, who was regularly in contact with the rebel camp, acting as a go-between, came to Blackheath surreptitiously on 7th June to find Cade fully in command and without challenge. This is much more in accord with the sounder theories for Cade's delay.

Cooke was an important link between the London supporters of Cade and Cade himself. He will be met again.

[3]

THE EMISSARIES who rode into the camp on the King's behalf were the Duke of Buckingham and the Archbishop of

Canterbury, attended by their followers (a small number). Humphrey Stafford, Earl of Stafford, had been created Duke of Buckingham in 1444. His mother, Anne, had married Edmund, Earl of Stafford, but during her life had become, on the death of her brother, the existing earl, Countess of Buckingham in her own right. Buckingham does not appear to have been a man of particular ability, and speedily fades from the clouded picture of these events.

John Stafford, Archbishop of Canterbury, was another member of the powerful Stafford clan, and probably lent a benign dignity to the proceedings in Cade's tent, while at the same time concealing beneath a calm exterior the shrewdness and cold clarity of an able administrator.

It is only fair to indicate that the source of the following version of what happened is Holinshed, who, as suggested in the Introduction, is not the most trustworthy of authorities. His account has here, however, a certain convincing quality, and is not contradicted in this respect by any other of the chronicles. It is reasonable to suppose, therefore, that it bears some relation to the truth.

The emissaries rode into the camp and were courteously received. Far from being the ignorant impostor portrayed by Shakespeare, Cade was found and reported by them to be a man temperate in both demeanour and speech, but in no mood to be browbeaten, and determined to show no servility. He was firm, but without arrogance. His army, he said, would disperse or retreat as soon as the King himself could be persuaded to come to Blackheath, hear the Kentish case, and concede the just demands of the insurgents.

Cade was now in complete command of his men, with power over their lives, and he showed clearly that he was entering into negotiation with these appointed or self-appointed emissaries as an equal, if not a superior. He and his leading advisers had now had time to draw up a detailed charter, setting forth their grievances and demands. The draft of this was shown or read to the royal messengers, and is said to have been ready, several days before their arrival, on the 4th June. It has been rightly claimed that this document, the contents of which are extant, is the best account we possess of the sufferings of the people during the earlier years of Henry VI's reign, and especially of those who made up the bulk of the insurgents.

The 'Bill of Complaints and Requests of the Commons of Kent', as it was entitled, is in its wording neither extreme, insolent, nor unduly rhetorical, but gives indication of having been drawn up by a man or body of men with a complete knowledge of the administrative and economic ills of England, and of Kent in particular. The document, widely circulated during the ensuing weeks, was couched in the somewhat antique language of the period. Those who prefer to study it in its original wording are referred to Appendix II. In the following lines the various points have been rewritten in the language of our own day, and their background has been briefly explained for the benefit of the ordinary reader. There is, however, some question whether the version carried back to London by the envoys of the Court was as moderate as this.

These, then, were the complaints and requests in the order given by their author.

1. It had been rumoured that as revenge for the assassination of the Duke of Suffolk, the county of Kent was to be laid waste and turned into 'a wild forest'.

William de la Pole, Duke of Suffolk, was commonly believed to have been far too friendly to the French, but his negotiation of a truce designed to last for two years to some extent restored him to popularity. However, doubts were reawakened when he married King Henry to Margaret of Anjou, because one condition of the arrangement was the abandonment of Maine and Anjou, English possessions. Suffolk agreed to this with reluctance, but from the moment this surrender of territory became common knowledge, hatred for him was revived.

It had earlier been alleged that he had instigated the murder of Humphrey, Duke of Gloucester, one of his greatest rivals, and there was abiding resentment among the Lancastrian party when he placed the Duke of Somerset, a Yorkist, in command of the army in France.

Suffolk had been made a Duke in July, 1448, and for a time remained in power unchallenged, but in much the same way as Chamberlain was deceived by Hitler at Munich, so he was deceived by the King of France, who, in the following March, broke the truce. The temporarily arrested war had to be resumed, and when defeat after defeat led to the total loss of Normandy, a prized realm of the Crown, Suffolk, again like Chamberlain, was reviled and lampooned. The rage of the English, in fact, produced such intolerable pressure upon those held responsible that Adam Molyneux (Moleyns or Molins), Bishop of Chichester, was compelled to resign. He had been Lord Treasurer of the State, and in Portsmouth a few days later, was assassinated by a body of furious seamen who slew him at the altar. The hostility to Suffolk now rose to such heights that although the Duke defended himself with great ability in Parliament, he was exiled by the King for a period of five years.

Suffolk sailed from England on 1st May, 1450, but in passage his ship was brought-to in the English Channel off Dover by a ship *Nicholas of the Tower*. He was dragged on board the interceptor, and on the following day his head was severed from his body. Although the *Nicholas* was a royal vessel, there is little doubt that this assassination was the work of Yorkist elements. Not unnaturally, Kent feared that a savage revenge would be taken upon the county as a whole. Rumours to this effect had evidently been put about, but with what justice it is impossible to decide.

2. The King had been forced to draw his income from the commoners, as the Crown revenues were being appropriated by 'other men'. This was making His Majesty a

The 'White Hart' inn, Southwark, Cade's temporary headquarters
(This picture shows the inn rebuilt after the Great Fire)

Medieval Blackheath, where Cade's army camped prior to the attack on London

An artist's reconstruction of fifteenth-century Cheapside

London Bridge, from an early print

poor man, and was the cause of heavy taxes which had to be paid by the people.

The 'other men' were, of course, the King's favourites, the spongers and hangers-on of the Court.

3. The Privy Council was being run by men not of royal blood, so that rampant corruption among judges and sheriffs alike was prevalent. As a result, people had to come with 'bribes and gifts' if they wished to obtain justice from the Council.

The Privy Council was a much more important body in those times than it is today. It was the real seat of government, the instrument by which the will of the Establishment percolated through to even the smallest town and village. The Privy Council had only to speak the word, and you were doomed to whatever punishment was considered necessary, whether or not your crime was a real one or merely a trumped-up charge. (It is not surprising that out of it grew the Star Chamber.) But it had a useful function. It acted as a primitive court of appeal, in that anyone whose lands had been filched from him, who had been perjured in local courts, who had been oppressed by tyrannous officials, or who had been falsely accused, whether of stealing a purse or leading a riot, could take his case to the Privy Council – on one condition. He must have 'a friend at Court' to take his side when the matter was heard.

It is plain that before a man could get justice, he had to be prepared to pay heavily for this kind of support. He could expect no impartiality among those who tried his case, either in his local courts or at the seat of power. What is more, he could not even sleep soundly of nights unless he had a sufficiently powerful protector at headquarters to ensure that he was not molested, murdered, robbed.

This was obnoxious to the commoners, and it formed one of their most bitter complaints.

D

4. Materials bought for the King's household under the 'Right of Purveyance' were not being paid for.

The 'Right of Purveyance' was, as earlier stated, the right of the King to be given food, drink and supplies, for both himself and his followers, whenever he went on journeys into the country. It was a custom of long standing, and was reasonable at the outset because it meant that the King was able to go about setting right popular wrongs and preventing the abuses liable to occur when authority is too remote. It had, however, by Cade's time, become sorely burdensome. Maintenance for the King had come to mean not only feeding and lodging him and his followers, but also providing expensive means of transport, such as horses and wagons, while even men were sometimes pressed into his service, being taken for the purpose from their own employment. Not only this, but the King's *family* claimed equal privileges.

It had always been understood that whatever was supplied to the visiting monarch should be properly recorded and paid for at a fair price, but in 1450 payment was seldom made, or else a 'tally' was handed to the supplier which enabled him to deduct the amount from his future tax levies, but this was often repudiated. The person whose business it was to arrange for these goods and services to be provided was known as the 'Purveyor'. He handed over a specification of the royal requirements, and at the same time – here was the rub! – fixed his own prices. Later, the name 'Purveyor' was changed to 'Buyer', but it did not make much difference.

5. Menials and others of the royal household stole the goods and lands of anyone impeached for treason before he had been convicted, and the accused men were unjustly held in prison, irrespective of their innocence or guilt, so that they were prevented from going to law to get their possessions restored.

This complaint requires no gloss, but is oddly reminiscent

of the happenings in the wild west of America during the periods of gold rush, claim-jumping, and railway development.

6. The poor and the commons of the realm, however genuine their title to their land, dared not defend it when unjustly challenged by the King's menial servants who coveted it.

This, again, is self-explanatory.

7. The loss of the King's territories in France (Normandy) was popularly said to be the result of treason by his lords and favourites, and an inquiry into the whole matter was urged, with death for the guilty as an example.

This is an interesting request, because without naming him, it obviously alludes to the death in unusual circumstances of the Duke of Gloucester. There was obviously great anger at the callous murder, as it was commonly regarded, of a popular leader who had been unjustly accused. An impartial inquiry, the insurgents believed, would beyond question reveal Lancastrian influence as responsible. It is, however, unlikely that Cade inserted this clause of his own accord. He can hardly have been so naïve as to imagine the King would initiate a proceeding likely to throw discredit upon himself and his advisers. It was either an expression of the insurgents' own intentions if they won their fight, or a cunning clause put in by Cade precisely because it would be unacceptable, and would therefore lead to war, so furthering his private ends. As suggested, however, this last reasoning appears somewhat far-fetched.

8. By reason of a writ, the Barons of the Kentish ports were exempt from collection of a special tax, but the unfortunate persons responsible for collecting the taxes had themselves to pay the legal expenses involved in this exemption.

The Cinque Ports had from the time of the Norman Conquest been exempted from a number of special taxes, and, indeed, from certain other taxes as well, but in Cade's day costs were charged against this exemption. Those entrusted with the general collection of taxes found that a proportion of these costs was debited to their account, and they had to pay it.

9. Sheriffs and under-sheriffs farmed out the collection of dues to the highest bidders, who then extorted excessive sums from the people.

This was no new complaint in human affairs. For centuries the taxes of China were fixed in just such a way. The Emperor's ministers decided how much he required, notified the Governors of Provinces what proportion of this total they had to supply, and the Governors then notified their under-lings how much they in turn must contribute to them individually. As long as each high official received the sum specified in advance, he did not ask how it had been obtained, nor what relation it bore to the capacity of the populace to pay it.

The one thing that can be said in favour of this system is that, after a fashion, it worked. The honourable tax-gatherers exacted what they felt to be a reasonable amount and sent it to the man higher up in the scale, after deducting their honest due. Others, however, were shameless, and then the people groaned under a burden that became almost unendurable.

10. Under the law by which hunting was taxable, poor men were taxed even when they did not hunt, and had to pay out of their own pockets bribes to those officials who had bought the power to collect the tax.

One can imagine the feelings of a modern man compelled to pay a tax for playing soccer when he did not know a goal-post from a lamp-post, and had never kicked a ball in his life; or, more accurately, perhaps, who was taxed for playing polo, which never in his life would he be able to afford. The practice of buying the right to collect taxes is also no new thing in history, and it was one of the grievances that brought about the revolutionary troubles in France at a later date. Governments were prepared to sell these rights because it saved them the expense of maintaining large staffs to supervise and exact. They knew before tax collection in any one year began just how much they would draw in, and once he had paid them it was the buyer's job to get it back with profit. How much he himself received was nobody's business but his own.

11. Lists were sent into the courts, and the men listed were held on trumped-up charges and fined whether guilty or not. It was argued that they had not complied with the orders of the court to attend, although they knew nothing about these orders, nor that they were called upon to defend themselves against the charges, of which they had not been notified.

These were the 'Writs of the Green Wax', which derived their name from the fact that the wax used for sealing them was green in colour. Allusion has earlier been made to these on page 27.

12. The Ministers of the Court of Dover annoyed and arrested people in their area on false pretexts and exacted heavy fees, a gross abuse of their local powers.

From this complaint we can discern the truth that many of the local Barons were little more than gangsters working a racket. You either paid the sum they demanded or you went to jail, and once in jail, who could say when, if ever, you would be released? It was better to pay up and look pleasant.

13. The people and tenants of Kent could not freely elect their representatives, but were compelled by pressure from the powerful to choose against their will those suggested to them.

There are parallels to this procedure familiar to those who have watched with aversion the practice of some of the states of Europe and elsewhere within living memory.

14. The Knights of Kent ought to choose the collectors of taxes on merit, but were now demanding gifts and bribes from those they choose.

15. The people were put to great trouble and expense because of the distance they had to travel to attend the Sessions, and therefore they wished the Sessions to be split up into two different centres, west and east, so that they could be more easily attended.

There now followed a list of Cade's demands, namely:

1. That the King himself shall rule, aided by loyal and favourable lords, and if this wish be granted, Cade declares that he and his men will fight and die for his cause.

This disproves the suggestion that Cade's insurrection was aimed at deposing the monarch and setting up a dictatorship in his place. It is possible that the demand was made tongue in cheek, but at this distance of time, we can but take the words at their face value. The 'loyal' lords were all probably Yorkist.

2. That the King shall renounce the false progeny and relations of the Duke of Suffolk, punish them by process of law, and substitute for them as his attendants the Duke of York, the Dukes of Exeter, Buckingham and Norfolk, and all the Earls and Barons.

3. That those who procured the death of the Duke of Gloucester, falsely accused of treason, be punished.

4. Cade points out the grievous losses of French territory for which these men were responsible, and the illustrious nobles on whom they brought unjust disgrace.

5. That extortion, the writs of green wax, the King's Bench depredations, the taking of provisions without pay-

ment, be ended, and that the Statute of Labourers be repealed or amended, and certain extortionate Kentish sheriffs be dismissed.

The Statute of Labourers was in actuality an accretion of laws designed to protect the community against unjust demands for wages and to ensure that labourers needed in their own district were not allowed to go elsewhere where they could earn more money. Any attempt of men to get together and protect themselves by agreeing on a fixed rate was prohibited. The justices of the district were not only empowered to decide all disputes between labourers and those who hired them, they could also decide what they should be paid. Men were press-ganged into working for the King wherever and whenever His Majesty desired and for whatever wage he chose to give.

You could not become apprenticed to a craft without first proving your possession of what was considered sufficient property. Otherwise a man whose station in life was low had to make his son a labourer. There was no 'educational ladder'. Only a few decades before Cade's rising had it become possible for schooling to be acquired by the common people without the risk of heavy fines upon the parents.

What all this amounted to was that no man could work where he liked, and had largely to take whatever he could get for his labour by bargaining, for which he was exceptionally ill-placed. There was a serious risk of imprisonment if he held out for a fair wage and refused to work for less.

Of course, the Statutes were difficult to enforce in their entirety. Men continually slipped away from one county to another to get better jobs, just as black slaves fled from South to North in the United States before slavery was abolished. The Statutes themselves were constantly being modified and tightened, fiddled with and tinkered at, but there is no doubting the exasperation and fury they aroused among the humble.

(There are modern parallels. In the U.S.S.R., as is well known, the Soviet citizen who wishes to work in Moscow cannot get into a train and travel there without a passport, which is granted only in exceptional circumstances. As a result there is always a floating population in the city who 'live black'. They have come in surreptitiously, and exist as best they can without a permit, hoping to escape notice.)

These, then were the famous Complaints and Demands. The reaction they produced in royal circles must now be considered.

[4]

THE ROYAL MESSENGERS probably rode at top speed back to Clerkenwell and their masters, carrying copies of the document they had received. It was not to be expected that this carefully-worded, restrained appeal, however reasonable and justified the changes it suggested, should be met with sympathetic consideration. In fact, in the hearts of its readers no generous response was aroused. For two days the Court considered the points raised, but there is no record whatsoever that at this stage any voice was heard in the insurgents' favour, or that any attempt was made to act upon their recommendations. Since they could not buy Cade off, the nobles and prelates now prepared for an overwhelming attack upon the camp at Blackheath.

On 17th June, the King officially commanded the rebels to disperse, and as a mark of contempt, returned no answer to the leader's demands. The general feeling among the royal party, as is usual when an underling makes himself a nuisance, was that the Captain of Kent would have to be taught a sharp lesson. If any suggestion of friendly response or even reasoned argument was ever put forward, it was dismissed as humiliating weakness. Violence was a much more popular remedy.

For purely selfish reasons some of the King's circle would

not have greatly minded the dismissal of the men named by Cade, but even these had no wish to adopt or see adopted the radical, far-reaching administrative and social reforms he advocated. With all the habitual contempt of those in power for those without it, they believed that those not 'of us' were 'agitators' without principle, were common, witless peasants born only to obey. The common people, to them, were – common.

FOUR

Battle at Solefields

[1]

MEANTIME, news of the rising had trickled through to the merchants and more enlightened citizens of London. The careful and temperate wording of the complaints and demands had become known, and the pledge of complete loyalty to the King if these were remedied convinced many of the 'reform party' that the proclamation was just and reasonable, its authors worthy of support. These men of property lost their first fears of assault by disorderly, rapacious hordes; secretly, there is little doubt, a few sympathisers slipped out of the city and made preliminary contact with the army at Black-heath. One of the most important of these was Thomas Cocke, or Cooke, one of Cade's licensed go-betweens.

Cooke had used his wealth to marry into the aristocracy. His daughter was now Lady Burghley, from whom the Cecils are said to be descended. This sinister character decided to insure himself against disaster by serving Cade while secretly conveying information about him to those who might find it useful.

Cade showed no sign of obeying the King's order to disperse his men, so the Court decided at last to march at once upon the rebels, King Henry in person at the head of his troops. On 17th June, the 'great lords', the King's masters in fact if not in name, rode through the streets of the city, helmets gleaming, ablaze with colour. Behind them file after file of hardened soldiers and newly-fledged recruits came tramping steadily along the cobbled ways. Ten thousand and more there were. None of their commanders doubted but that by nightfall they would have occupied the rebel camp and driven the broken Kentish levies helter-skelter before them down the Surrey tracks.

Perhaps from Cooke, perhaps from spies of his own, perhaps by message sent by his sympathisers in the city, Cade learned early of the intended advance of the King's forces. On the night of the 16th June, he broke camp and retired from the common for the reasons already suggested in the previous chapter. His withdrawal was executed in perfect order through Bromley and Chislehurst into the wooded country around Sevenoaks, where he planned to surprise the advancing royal army and defeat it in a battle or series of battles.

Sevenoaks (Senocke) is today a charming little town, dormitory for those working in London. It lies on a hill above the woods of the North Downs overlooking a valley through which flows a placid river. It had a special significance for the rebels because close by lay Knole (Knowle), the seat of the hated James Fiennes, Lord Treasurer and Lord Chamberlain, who had been created Lord Saye and Sele in 1447. He was one of those held largely responsible with Suffolk for the loss of Maine and Anjou.

As suggested earlier, Cade may have explained his retreat to Sevenoaks by holding out hopes of sacking the 'great grave house'. This would not only excuse his withdrawal, and give a fillip to his cause, but also show that the insurgents meant what they said. There would be an opportunity for loot as well as of avenging themselves upon one of their most loathed oppressors.

In fact, however, Knole never was sacked. Either the news of a rapid advance of the royal army left no time, or Cade changed his mind, or he had never had any intention of attacking his enemy's undefended house. Knole's square,

undecorated towers are there to this day. (The house was
sold by Saye's son, William, to Thomas Bourchier, Archbishop of Canterbury, in 1456, for £1,266 13s. 4d.)

As the retiring army once more marched through the
Kentish countryside, they were met by a disturbing silence.
The inns were virtually empty; the houses shuttered; the
pilgrims departed from Wrotham; but against this, bands of
peasants, headed by priests and singing the slanderous ditties
of the insurrection as they marched, came to join them. A
single gleam shines out of the medieval darkness to reveal the
firm hold Cade had upon his followers. At Sevenoaks, he
caused a squire of the name of Stanlaw to be beheaded,
probably for a breach of discipline, or for some offence against
the countryfolk. This throws considerable light upon the later
accusations brought against him, which shall be examined in
due time.

[2]

THE KING and the army reached Blackheath before nine
o'clock on the morning of 18th June. Here, baffled by the
desolation and silence where they had expected to meet rank
upon rank of furious peasantry, they paused. The deserted
camp puzzled them, and the leaders met to decide upon the
course to follow. The enemy's main position had been occupied; he was evidently in full retreat; but he was still very
much alive. It is never sufficient in warfare to take a position.
The enemy must be brought to battle and annihilated. There
was no question but that Cade must be pursued. The one
question was: What direction had he taken?

It was not difficult to answer. A guerrilla band can take to
the hills and woods in self-supporting handfuls; an organised
army such as Cade's is largely tied to the roads. It was
probably not difficult to discover the direction he had taken –
down the trunk road. Cade's week at Blackheath, however,

had denuded the region of supplies, and the probability that he would do all in his power to deny them to the pursuers had to be taken into account. Moreover, while it was good that the King should have ridden through the streets of London and come to Blackheath with his army, it would be foolish to carry him farther. It was believed that one of the rebel leader's objectives was to capture Henry himself, and so, by meeting him face to face, have the longed-for opportunity of pleading his cause in person.

For logistic and political reasons, therefore, it was decided that the major portion of the royal forces should remain at Blackheath and guard the King, while an effective, well-armed contingent under Sir Humphrey Stafford and William Stafford, Esquire, should follow hard on the heels of Cade and bring him to battle. The Staffords appear to have volunteered for this task, having motives of self-interest. According to one chronicler, their intention was to take this chance of enriching themselves by appropriating the lands of those they took it for granted they would defeat. There is reason to believe they were warned of the risks they ran, but these warnings they ignored. With their inferior force, advancing from Bromley, they either caught up with Cade or were allowed to catch up with him.

The main road through Sevenoaks past the entrance to Knole Park leads to a little suburb known as Solefields, which in those days was a tiny hamlet at the southern end of the town. Today it is the Park Grange Estate, a collection of small houses lying in an angle between the roads to Tonbridge and Sevenoaks Weald (as it is now labelled). One has only to trudge towards it from the town to perceive that it must have been an ideal site for ambush. The road here cuts sharply through steep, once thickly-wooded slopes, from which, hidden among the trees and the long grass above, the Kentish insurgents could pour arrows into the massed soldiery in the road below, and when they had been thrown into confusion and terror, rush down upon them with all the advantage of surprise.

It was at Solefields, or the Sole Field, that Cade awaited his pursuers.

The Staffords, members of an old Norman family of high distinction, were experienced soldiers, well-connected, and claiming kinship with the Duke of Buckingham and the Archbishop of Canterbury. They were contemptuous of the force they were about to meet, just as were the British generals of the Boers in South Africa before they discovered their worth as fighting men. After all, *they* were 'professionals', the enemy a motley array of country yokels led by a bastard from Ireland. They had not the slightest doubt of the result.

All unsuspecting they walked blindly into the trap. Caught in the bottleneck of the narrow road between the slopes, they were unable to escape the hail of arrows and the fierce charge that followed. Both the Staffords were killed and virtually the entire force annihilated. What few were left 'withdrew to prepared positions', as the classic phrase goes. In reality, they fled, a frightened, shattered mob. Some, their discipline collapsing under stress, plundered as they went the houses of the very nobles they had been sent to defend. Others joined Cade.

[3]

THE MAIN BODY of the King's army had by now accompanied him to Greenwich where, pending news from the Staffords, it had been deemed advisable he should go. A detachment or so may have remained at Blackheath to guard the approaches to London. What is certain is that when news of the lost battle was brought to the King, he was at Greenwich, whence he departed in some haste by water up the Thames to London, no doubt on the insistence of his advisers. They were not leaving him to be captured by a sudden raid or in danger of injury should Cade attack in strength. In all these decisions affecting the King's movements, the Queen had a considerable, probably the final, say. She was a woman of great spirit and dominating character.

Not so far away from Kenilworth in the Midlands were Thomas Stanley and Thomas Harington, prominent Lancastrians, who had been deputed by the royal party on 1st June to call up levies and assemble them at Chester and Lancaster, their respective centres. These were to be armed, drilled, and commanded by the officers in question, and held in readiness to move at any moment. On the news of Cade's victory, Lord Scales, Governor of the Tower, was commanded to retain under arms and hold at his disposal in the fortress any troops who had recently been shipped home from France for demobilisation. These, it was assumed, had had no time or opportunity to be contaminated by any mutineers in the city. Ordinary citizens who were physically fit and willing to fight in the King's defence were likewise to be enrolled and armed.

As a friendly gesture to the rebels, the Common Council of the City of London dismissed on 26th June that member of their body who had led the Court party among them – Philip Malpas – and whom in 1448 they had been compelled against their will to elect to the Aldermanic bench. Malpas lived at the Green Gate in Cornhill, and like Thomas Cooke, was a draper. He had represented the City in Parliament in 1439– 1440, and was a staunch Lancastrian, owing his position entirely to the Lancaster influence. Yet there is ground for the belief that he, too, had had secret dealings with the Duke of York. It was the way of commercial men in those days of faction and feud to keep a foot in both camps. (Malpas died in 1469, and was one of the survivors of the last big battle of the Cade rising.)

[4]

CADE APPEARS to have made it clear in some way after his victory that as his demands had been rejected and he had been compelled to fight, nothing less than the surrender of the city would now satisfy him. In consequence the King was badly frightened. On the 30th June he ordered Lord Scales, Governor of the Tower of London, to guard the prisoners in his keeping, and also signed an order for the arrest of Lord Saye as a sop to the angry murmurs of which he had been told. Saye was apprehended in his presence and sent to the Tower that same day.

Henry was still in London on the 28th June, because he is known to have signed a treaty there on that day. Nevertheless, Saye's imprisonment did not subdue the continual murmurs of the Yorkist faction. Even some of the members and nobles of his own household, including Lord Dudley, began to insist that something must be done to meet Cade's demands.

One unexpected effect of the battle of Solefields was an almost complete loss of control over the royal forces. Many of the men-at-arms drifted away from Greenwich, shouting and jeering, and came flooding into London, where they united with the Cade faction to burn and pillage the houses of certain execrated or absent courtiers. They clamoured also for judgement on the Abbot of Gloucester and other leading potentates, including John Norice and Jon Terhune, whom they accused of oppression. These men, however, had not stayed to await condemnation, but had taken time by the top-knot and fled post-haste to their manors and estates in the country.

The now terrified Henry decided to save his royal skin and leave his capital, putting himself and his Queen and Court well out of reach of the advancing rebels. The Lord Mayor of London and his Councillors pleaded with him to remain in the city, even offering to support the entire cost of his household, but they pleaded in vain. The King withdrew, with remnants of his army who had remained loyal, to Berk-hampstead, as far as which town they accompanied him. Their number is unknown. Here he sheltered for two or three days in the castle of Robert of Mortain, of which today only

HENRICUS.VI. *Angl: & Fr: Rex.*
Coll: *Regalis* Cantab: A.º *1443 Fund.*
et Etonia A.º D.ⁿⁱ 1443 Fundator
c Effigiem Rev.ᵈ° Viro H:Godolphin STP & Coll: *Etoniensis Præpositi*
Humillime Dicat J.Faber

Henry VI, whose honest but weak character helped bring about the insurrection

A priest named John Ball did much to rouse the people to Wat Tyler's aid

Lord Saye and Sele is brought before Jack Cade and sentenced to death. From a drawing by Charles Lucy of an engraving by W. Ridgway

the earthworks and a few clumps of fallen masonry are left
to mark the position of the original walls.

Even Berkhampstead was not felt to be safe enough.
Farther north were more trustworthy forces and the levies of
Stanley and Harington. There may even have been a doubt
whether those soldiers who had followed the King from
London were to be relied upon if Cade attacked. Leaving the
citizens of London to fend for themselves, therefore, the
royal body moved on, to Kenilworth Castle.

E

FIVE

Return to Blackheath

[1]

KING HENRY VI, who had come to the throne in 1421, and was to reign, more by luck than judgement, for fifty years, was the son of that bellicose warrior, Henry V, idol of Shakespeare in his day and of the English in all generations since. A mere babe when he came to the throne, he had at the outset the advantage of being under the guardianship of his scholarly and cautious uncle, Cardinal Beaufort. As he grew up, it became plain that his character was totally different from that of his father. Quiet, pacific, almost pusillanimous, conditioned by his too early accession to look to his guardian and advisers for counsel, he was essentially a man of peace. But peace was the last thing most of his people wanted.

In the end he was the victim both of his own character and of the intense rivalries and ambitions of two great houses, those of York and Lancaster. A young man when rebellion broke out, he had neither the will nor the intelligence to see in it as Richard II had done, a means of securing a greater personal hold on his country and her subjects.

It was a misfortune for him that when the Cardinal died, he should have had to accept as his chief adviser the indiscreet, though honest, Duke of Suffolk, whose death left him the pawn of rival factions.

Not personally popular, except among his immediate

friends and supporters, he won distinction by neither military nor political brilliance. He had no great achievements to his name. On the contrary, his reign had brought to a harassed nation nothing but hardship, humiliation and disaster, with which and its accompanying misrule they came inevitably to identify him. It is not surprising, therefore, that his advisers should have deemed him unsafe while ever he lay within the reach of the rebels.

The departure, of the King from their midst despite all their protests, was a blow to the loyal townsmen, because it not only removed from the city of London a rallying point and buttress, the royal presence, with all the mystic fervour it generated, but also the main force with which to withstand a rebel assault. They found themselves virtually defenceless. Nevertheless, it has never been the way of Englishmen to be abject in face of disaster. The citizens decided to do what they could for themselves. It is an intriguing thought that had the King remained with his people in this crisis, the wars of the Roses might never have taken place. His popularity would have been so greatly enhanced, his face and figure been so much better known, that he might have been encouraged to dominate his lords and give England the wise rule and generous treatment she sorely needed. But the King fled to Kenilworth, and the chance was lost.

The one trustworthy defence left to London was the Tower of London, which contained both troops and guns. (On 13th June the sum of one hundred pounds had been set aside for the defence of the Tower.) Abandoned by King, Lords of Council, and all the nominal authority of the land, the Lord Mayor of London, Charlton by name, at first refused to offer resistance to the rebels if they invaded the city. He had some excuse, for the nobles, as panic-stricken as he, had almost all escaped to their castles in the provinces; but his threat had left the King unmoved.

Once again, Thomas Cocke or Cooke makes one of his furtive appearances. Well before the decisive battle of Solefields, Cooke, as Cade's envoy, had been going in and out of his camp, as is known, with a proper safeguard. His basic purpose was to raise money for the present and future needs of the insurgents. During the 10th to 13th June, he came again to London, where he was one of the four Wardens of the Drapers' Society, as well as a Member of Parliament. We shall learn presently on what business he came.

[2]

THE RICH PRIZE of England's greatest city lay now virtually defenceless at Cade's feet, but once more, the general, so active in the field, allowed precious days to pass and the impact of his victory to weaken. He did not re-occupy his old camp at Blackheath until the 29th June, St Peter's Day. Nevertheless, there may have been justification for this. He needed, perhaps, to whip up local enthusiasm for his cause, to draw fresh money and recruits from the east of Kent and the county of Sussex. Whether this be so or not, it proved to be a serious error. These things could have waited. They were less important than to secure an unshakeable hold on the centre of the country's trade and administration. In fact, surveying Cade's career as a whole, it will be plain that these unexplained procrastinations more than any other factor were the seed of his later disasters.

It is sometimes claimed that he spent the period between the 11th and 29th June in remedying a number of local injustices for which the Duke of Suffolk's influence had been responsible. Among these are said to have been the restoration of seized lands to their rightful owners, the removal of corrupt justices from office, and a personal appearance in some of the districts from which he had drawn support. He went, in effect, to 'show the flag', and put fresh heart into the waverers and those who 'sat on the fence' despite their essential sympathy with his cause.

There is, in fact, some evidence for this in an Act of Parliament of 1592, which expressly undid whatever had been done during the rising. There is also a document, which will be more extensively referred to later, suggesting that its author, in his endeavour to make contact with Cade during this period, was forced to travel from point to point in Kent and Sussex. Maidstone and Tonbridge are especially mentioned in this connection. Another who appears to have sought him in various parts was Andrew Hooles or Hulles, Keeper of the Privy Seal, sent to interview him.

Even when, in the end, he reoccupied the camp at Blackheath, Cade allowed himself to be delayed in his march on London by one of the oldest tricks in history: the offer to negotiate. But before the story is told of his second meeting with envoys of the King, it must be recorded how greatly the Captain of Kent's position had been strengthened by his victory, his appearances in various districts unchallenged and unattacked, and the propaganda he and his supporters had made before and after Solefields.

[3]

MEANWHILE, reports of the apparently decisive success of the leader in his first clash with the armies of authority had kindled a blaze throughout southern and south-eastern England. East Sussex now came out strongly in his support, and the local constables called up their men in the accredited manner, using the muster rolls of the county. These they despatched with arms and provisions to Cade at Blackheath. Volunteers had previously set off to join up with him before being formally summoned by their constables. The names of at least 400 Sussex men who took part in the rising are on record, and from eight parishes came every available man. Among the leaders of this contingent were John Danyel Prior of Lewes; Richard Dartmouth, Abbot of Battle, and among the landed gentry such names appear as the Apsleys, the Bartletts, Bartholomew Bolner, who had lived in the Manor of West Firle for over ten years, the Burtons, Chaloners, Colbrons, and many others. Two landowners, twenty-three country gentlemen, with yeomen, bailiffs and clerks, came from Lewes, Seaford and Pevensey.

In some cities of the south serious rioting broke out, and in Wiltshire, in particular, one of the more ignoble ecclesiastics, William Ayscough, Bishop of Salisbury, was assailed on 29th June after celebrating mass at his Manor of Edyndon in Wiltshire, torn struggling from the altar of his church, stabbed to death, and his naked body flung into the fields, while his home was ruthlessly sacked. Officers of the royal household who had left London for the safety of their country homes were attacked, and narrowly avoided the same fate.

Surrey had also been won over to some extent, and beyond doubt drafts from this somewhat lukewarm county were present at Blackheath. More important than this, however, if proper use had been made of it, was the uprising of the men of Essex, to whom Cade had sent messengers advising them of the disruption of the royal army and his impending march on London. The Essex band set off immediately on their long march.

It is surprising that so little has come down to us concerning this Essex advance, which could have changed the entire course of English history. They had certainly a commander, vaguely alluded to in the Chronicles as a 'Captain', and equally certain they endeavoured to co-ordinate their progress with that of Cade, so that both armies should enter London together. It is clear that they came within striking distance of the battle that was to follow, but after getting as far as Mile End, and even meeting Cade, for some unexplained reason they halted. All the records are silent as to their fate thereafter. They came, they saw, but they did not conquer. Instead, they vanished into the dark waters of unwritten history.

One cannot resist unrewarding speculation as to their

motives and actions. The most kindly explanation is that after their long forced march, they needed rest, and were in no condition for fighting. By the time they were ready to move again, it was too late. Events had overtaken them. They may have lingered hopefully for a few days, keeping alive the dying belief that things might yet go well. But when they saw that their cause was lost, and while the Londoners were too preoccupied with Cade and his men to pay them much attention, they quietly slipped away to their homes, possibly as a body, possibly in one's and two's at first, then in increasing numbers, thankful for the lucky chance that had saved their lives and possessions. The truth is, we do not know.

On the other hand, less favourable explanations can be conceived. The Essex men, fresh from their relatively primitive fishing villages and marshes, may have succumbed to the fleshpots of the capital, and been in no condition for serious warfare. They may have been less disciplined and less well-equipped than the Kentish bands, and consequently unable or disinclined to challenge the terrifying might of the Tower, plainly before them. Or they may – who knows? – have made their way secretly by a devious route to Southwark and participated with Cade's men in the battle that eventually settled the argument. The first explanation seems, however, the more probable.

We shall assume, therefore, that they did *not* spend their time in drinking, wenching and looting, while time went by. We shall assume that their leaders did not lose control, and that what had been a well-ordered force did not at once disintegrate into a disorderly mass. But there, bivouacked at Mile End, we must leave them unwept, unhonoured and unhung.

[4]

THE MAIN RESPONSIBILITY for the failure of the Essex men to play a serious part in Cade's progress must rest with the leader himself. By the time he was ready to occupy London, bands of his enthusiastic allies were assembling and moving towards the city from Sussex, Surrey, Essex, Suffolk and Middlesex. He allowed them to dribble in without any coherent plan of campaign, and appears to have moved throughout the decisive opening days of July without reference to their whereabouts or intentions, except those of the Essex men.

What is worse, while he himself was anxious not to frighten the more influential of London's citizens by allowing acts of lawlessness, and did not hesitate to have another unimportant officer of his army executed for disobedience, he did not publicly or privately disown the abominable murder of the Bishop of Salisbury. Nor did he reprove other outbreaks of violence in various parts of the south.

There were, for example, armed risings in Portsmouth, Winchester, Norwich and Coventry, and there is reason to believe that the Yorkists helped to foment these disturbances, though the Duke of York had no part in Cade's rebellion, from which, indeed, he suffered a small loss as the records reveal.

Unfortunately, Cade's name was freely used by the instigators and leaders of these riots, as if they were desired and approved by him. On the contrary, they were bad for his cause, weakening the belief that once in control he would be able to restrain his followers and act generously and well towards the conquered. It would have been statesmanlike to disavow these outbreaks and to punish or promise punishment of the offenders, while recompensing those unjustly afflicted. But acts of statesmanship were rare in medieval times. He did not. The state of mind of rulers and generals was altogether different from that of today. It is known, however, that Cade caused Parys, one of his officers, to be beheaded for larceny of some kind.

[5]

WHILE CADE is lingering in his tent at Blackheath, it is necessary to return to Thomas Cooke and his activities. This man was once more acting as an authorised negotiator on Cade's behalf with his many supporters in London. Because Cade was now militarily the master of the entire south, Cooke worked for him with enthusiasm. His career gives a noteworthy indication of his character.

Becoming eventually Sheriff of London in 1453, five years after Philip Malpas – earlier mentioned in this account – had achieved his Aldermanship, he became Alderman of the Ward of Vintry at the instigation of King Edward IV after the Lancastrian victory at St Albans. In 1461 he was elected Lord Mayor of London, and became a Member of Parliament in 1462-63. The son-in-law of Malpas, he was knighted in 1465 at the Coronation of Queen Elizabeth, wife of Edward IV, former Duke of York and Earl of March. Cooke built the front only of Gidea Hall (occupied during World War I by the Artists' Rifles Cadet Corps), the main portion of this house being completed by his descendants.

In 1467, Cocke (Cooke) was accused of high treason and imprisoned in the Tower, but when tried at the Guildhall, was found not guilty, though compelled to pay fines totalling £18,800. He lost his office of Alderman in the following year, but regained it on the 13th October, 1471. After the battle of Tewkesbury and the upheavals of that turbulent period, he fled to France, was intercepted by a ship from the Low Countries and once more jailed. He died in 1478, an intriguer and fomenter of mischief, defeated in life by his own character. He is described as bold of speech, quick-witted and well-respected. It may be said of him that too many such Cookes would spoil any nation's broth.

[6]

IT HAS BEEN indicated that there was some desire among the more timorous members of the Common Council to admit the Captain of Kent and his forces without opposition. In this way, it was suggested, bloodshed and the destruction of valuable property, inevitable if fighting broke out, would be avoided. Moreover, the commander would be better able to keep his men in check if they had no injuries to avenge. This argument was certainly inspired by naked self-interest rather than compassion or altruism, but its advocates were all the more passionate for precisely this reason.

Cade, however, had more in view than terms of surrender. He was in urgent need of money and arms and meant to get them. His most cunning stroke as a politician was to demand them through Cooke, and perhaps at his suggestion, from that body which would be the easiest to despoil, and whose spoliation would least offend and alarm the merchants and city fathers.

Cooke's formal safe-conduct from Cade for this purpose reads : 'By this our writing ensealed, we grant and will permit truly, that Thomas Cocke, of London, draper, shall come in good surety and in safeguard to our presence and to avoid from us again at his pleasure, with all other persons assigned at his denomination with him coming in likewise'.

London was the home of the Lombards and other foreign traders, such as the Venetians and the Florentines. These he ordered to provide at once six fully-saddled and bridled horses, twelve battleaxes, twelve swords, twelve first-rate harnesses, twenty-four brigandines or coats of light and pliable mail armour (though these may have been pairs of greaves). It appears possible that these were intended for his principal officers. He also demanded one thousand marks, not in bankers' order or promissory notes, but in hard cash – a sum amounting to approximately £700. If these demands were refused, their heads would fall the moment he became lord of the city.

One may picture the wily, double-dealing Cooke presenting these alternatives without explicit threat, but with a significant movement of the hand towards his neck and a glance that had no pity.

The Lombards, energetic and able bankers and merchants, who had been established in England since the 13th century, and gave our language the phrase 'lumber room', were of foreign extraction, but not all of them were from Lombardy itself. They were therefore much more susceptible to black-mail than their English counterparts, who disliked them and feared their competition. The knowledge that these foreigners would have to pay the rebel army for their protection in no way harmed Cade with the Londoners. On the contrary, it suggested to the men who mattered in the city that if he became their master, England would be once more for the English alone, and 'Lombards go home!' would become a popular slogan.

That the Lombards gave way is virtually certain because there is no indication that any of them suffered harm or were victims of mob violence in the tumult of the next few days, though this, of course, is but negative evidence.

SIX

Cade in London

[1]

THE COMMON COUNCIL, under pressure from Cade through Cooke, discussed his entry into the city. The Aldermen and Councillors were by no means unanimous on whether to admit him without opposition or to give battle in an attempt to preserve the city from capture. It was therefore agreed that they should meet as a body in the Guildhall, and come to a formal decision on 3rd July.

Learning through Cooke of the meeting convened, Cade again allowed himself to be put off and waited for the result, instead of marching without more ado. Thus, the day came, and the meeting duly took place with but one item on the agenda: resistance or surrender?

The rich merchants of English blood had had no objection to Cade's successful blackmailing of the Lombards, even though it strengthened his force. Competition from these foreigners had been hitting them hard, and in consequence, the Lombards were disliked both by their rivals and by the ordinary citizens. On the other hand, some of these bourgeois Englishmen had been of the party of the Duke of Suffolk, and had paid him large sums for their protection. These feared lest Cade should demand even heavier sums, while his proffered protection might be even less effective.

Cade himself was convinced that his whole insurrection

would prove abortive unless he succeeded in shaking up and reforming the administration in London. Until this had been achieved, he could not hope to control the country as a whole, and his ambition grew with his success, so he came more and more to regard this control as his right. (His use of the royal 'we' in the safe-conduct given to Cooke will not be overlooked.)

The discussion lasted for some hours, and it can be conceived that much ill-temper and many recriminations accompanied it. A decision was reached at last, however, and the Lord Mayor, whose threat to Henry to abandon the city if he should desert his subjects will be recalled, played now a part entirely different from what this might have led his colleagues to suppose. He spoke with the utmost vigour demanding that Cade should be barred from the city, by force of arms, if necessary. Active measures should at once be taken to oppose him. Thus, he completely reversed his earlier position.

Nevertheless, the departure of their sole effective military protector – since the handful of troops in the Tower could not be expected to take offensive action – was too much for the great majority of the Councillors. With but one exception, they voted that the gates should be thrown open as soon as the insurgents presented themselves.

Before this decision could be reached there was a delay, because no justices could be found to start the proceedings in the proper legal fashion. Outside the Guildhall there was muttering and booing from the populace, eager for Cade, and if any of the justices were left in London, they took good care to keep away. In the end, however, one justice braver than the rest, Robert Danvers, whose name deserves to be remembered, was found and did what was necessary.

The Council, having made up their minds, now proceeded to show willing by indicting several of the leaders of the King's party, including the Suffolks, Danyell and Saye, but left their property intact until they had been brought to trial and a verdict of guilty delivered.

The one man present who (assuming the Lord Mayor to have abstained from voting, as Chairman) opposed the surrender was Robert Horne, a fishmonger by trade, who spoke eloquently against what he doubtless described in blunt Billingsgate language as treachery, treason, disloyalty, betrayal of the King. This speech gave great offence to the remaining members of the Council, and he was forthwith flung into Newgate jail, or, as the record has it, 'put in ward'.

We can be sure that Cooke, if he did not take the news himself, lost no time in despatching a messenger to Cade telling him of the decision. This time Cade moved. Breaking up his camp at Blackheath, he marched into Southwark, on the south bank of the Thames, and before long his men were looking across the river at the great city which seemed to have held them from it for weary weeks. There, before their eyes, was London Bridge, lined with the mean houses of the time, huddled together, and beyond could be seen the Tower, a dark menace, silent now, but capable of roaring with violence through the mouths of her cannon. Beyond, too, lay the great warehouses lining the wharves, the houses of the hated nobles, the taverns and delights. For this they had marched, drilled, fought, waited: they had reached their journey's end.

Between them and London now lay only the bridge. Cade is said to have ridden across it on a good horse – perhaps one of those extorted from the Lombards – and to have entered the city at five o'clock that same afternoon. The drawbridge had been let down, and the keys of the bridge had already been handed over to him. Behind him as he rode came men whose immediate task was to sever the ropes of the drawbridge so that it could not be raised again treacherously after he had moved into the city, or by any 'resistance movement' trying to cut off his retreat should he be attacked and defeated.

[2]

IT IS NOT without advantage to pause for a moment and consider the men to whom we owe such accounts as have come down to us of the events of 1450. For the most part they were ordinary townsmen watching from their windows and noting down what they saw and heard, or what was said to have been heard. It is clear that some among them, being permanently located in the city, could have little notion of the root causes of the revolt. (Londoners during industrial disputes in our own age have been heard to express opinions betraying surprising ignorance of their genesis. Particularly is this the case when the dispute in question occurs in, for example, the mines of South Wales or the steelworks of Sheffield.)

Here and there, however, little touches reveal that they described what they themselves saw, what did in fact occur, but where they merely write down the tittle-tattle of the alley or the market-place they cannot always be relied upon. They knew with fair accuracy what was occurring in the city itself, but were inclined to guess at the rest. In assessing their evidence we have to keep in mind, as earlier remarked, that many were Lancastrians and unable to believe that Cade's revolt had honourable motives or that he himself was any other than an impostor. Even the neutrals, when all was over, needed to be discreet in their comments for fear of pro-scription.

Confirmation can sometimes be found in official documents of the period, but for the most part the historian can but weigh each statement against the rest and endeavour to achieve a fair and impartial judgement. Thus, some Chronicles assert that Cade marched into London on the 1st July, whereas others favour the 2nd or 3rd. The exact dates seem to this writer unimportant. The essential fact is that Cade entered London during the first two or three days of July and became its Lord.

[3]

ACCORDING TO THE CHRONICLES, he 'rode in every street like
a lordly captain', dressed in the clothing and in the armour
studded with gilt nails that had belonged to Sir Humphrey
Stafford, slain at Solefields. He wore gilt spurs, a gilt 'salat',
or helmet, and over the armour, a gown of blue velvet, all
probably acquired from his fallen enemy. The narrow streets
were packed with a cheering mob, among whom were, unquestionably, those parasites upon victorious revolutionaries,
the greedy slum-dwellers and unemployed soldiery, eager to
burn, loot, steal, rape, even kill, if opportunity offers, and to
avenge themselves upon an enemy or remove an obstacle to
their desires.

It can readily be conceived that Cade would have great
difficulty in bringing his men through the howling, shoving
mob, but he had presence and authority, and in his passage
down one thoroughfare after another, he was careful to
preserve the reputation he had won for good discipline among
his troops. He knew too well how much depended upon the
first impression his army made upon the citizens to allow the
order and high purpose of his revolt to be disrupted.

Whenever held up by the press of sweating bodies, he
addressed the crowd, while meantime his officers and sergeants
cleared a way. He took upon himself to declare that he came
as a loyal supporter of the King, and that his occupation of
London did not mean that robbery, pillage, and other
offences, were to follow. On the contrary, he expressly
promised the instant execution of any found misbehaving,
looting, or offending the peaceful. In view of his later words
that day, however, it is difficult not to believe that he had his
tongue in his cheek when he added that in taking such action
he would be acting in the King's name.

A chronicler has recorded that the first of these speeches
was delivered at St Magnus, close to London Bridge.
Another was made at Leadenhall as Cade began his ride

Jack Cade declares himself Lord of London on July 2, 1450

The burning of St John's Monastery near Smithfield by Wat Tyler's men

through the city proper. Then came an incident standing out like a scarlet blot on a fair page, an incident that Shakespeare has used with enormous dramatic effect in his play, and that possesses the touch of 'panache', of showmanship, which history and the people love. It was, moreover, the clearest indication that Cade no longer saw himself in terms of an armed petitioner to a revered monarch, but as himself England's destined leader. He had taken London, and was now virtually its lord and England's king.

Possibly this remarkable flourish, this mystical tribute to a superstition, is a legend, a fairy-tale for the delectation of children, designed to make their learning of English history more palatable; but few believe this. There is too much testimony to the act. Even the location of the incident is given.

As Cade was riding through the city streets, he came to a now forgotten thoroughfare known as Canyutke, Canwick or Candlewick Street (now Cannon Street). There before him stood the famous, almost sacred Stone of London. London Stone was revered as having from the earliest times been the focal point of assembly for those legislators who governed the city, and for the receiving of petitions from suitors. All public proclamations and collective summonses were here delivered, and what is more, debts contracted and payments made. Merchants made it their meeting-place and in its shadow regulated their affairs.

Sir Christopher Wren considered it to be part of a monument in the forum of Londinium, erected during the Roman occupation, and others have supposed it to be a 'millarium' or central point for the measurement of distance. There is another theory that the Stone was originally a house of stone built by the elective Lord of London, Fitzaylwin, after the great fire of London in the reign of King Stephen. The use of stone instead of timber for houses was then unusual enough to have made an example of it both conspicuous and impressive because of its cost, strength and greater security from fire.

F

Such a house is known to have existed, and was either the first or the largest of its kind. There is a record of it as late as 1240 A.D., when it was occupied by John de Londonston.

In the third decade of the fifteenth century the first reference to London Stone in Canwick Street occurs in the verses of a poet, Lifgate. The Stone of Cade's day may have been a relic of or connected with Fitzaylwin's house by standing on the same site.

However, the consensus of opinion is that the stone was of pre-historic origin, and as such, endowed with magical qualities, so that any declaration made after contact with it in the manner adopted by Cade, doubtless following a tradition with which he was familiar, had a significance this age may find it difficult to understand. In effect it gave to his words the force and value of an oath and at the same time the certainty that they would be fulfilled. For all but the sceptical, therefore, Cade declared himself as, and was certain to be, legislator-in-chief and future King when, jumping off his horse, he walked to the Stone, took his sword from his swordbearer, struck the Stone with great force, seated himself upon it, and in the presence of the Lord Mayor, Sir Thomas Charlton, and a seething, jostling assembly of citizens, uttered the potent words: '*Now is Mortimer lord of this city!*'

Though he did not explicitly say so, there could be no doubt now where Cade stood. Give a few more victories like Solefields, and a new dynasty would be founded and its founder rule England. Doubtless Charlton heard this audacious declaration with feelings of alarm and depression, because this ceremony was no meaningless piece of braggadocio. To him as to the populace it had a genuine, spine-chilling significance.

It is not commonly known that a London Stone is still in existence, though there is no certainty that it is in any way connected with the original. This one was found in the 1870s 'hidden under a bushel', and was uncovered by members of the London and Middlesex Archaeological Society. Little is known of the history of this ancient piece, but it was obviously oolitic stone that had been used for building. This led some of the members to believe it the last remaining fragment of the old stone house, and therefore the original London Stone.

The London Stone struck by Cade was, then, a real stone, and existed on the same site as late as John Stow, the historian (1525-1605). Whether its size had diminished over the centuries is unknown, but it has always been the subject of great interest, as the various theories regarding its origin show.

[4]

BY THE TIME Cade had finished his procession through the city, it was becoming dark. He took the Lord Mayor aside and conferred with him as to the measures to be taken to maintain order in the city, the leave to be granted to his men so that they might come and go to and from Southwark as they wished and were permitted, or their duties necessitated. Also discussed were such mundane matters as water, provisions and lodging for any bodies of men he himself saw fit to quarter within the gates of the city. This done and agreement reached, Cade withdrew over London Bridge and went back to his camp in Southwark. Here he made his headquarters at a famous hostelry: the White Hart Inn (some call it the White Horse Inn).

The inns of Southwark belonged mostly to southern religious houses such as St Augustine's of Canterbury, the Priory of Lewes and Hyde Abbey, and were situated in many instances at the nearest point to the entrance gates.

The White Hart is perhaps one of the most famous British inns in history. The illustration shows the building as it was in 1670, but this is not the inn that housed the Captain of Kent, which was burned down by accident in 1669, when a great fire raged in Southwark. At that time the tenant was

Robert Baynton, and the landlord or property holder, John Collett. The rebuilt White Hart was, however, similar to because largely a copy of the old. Even the 'new' inn has now disappeared, but it is interesting to note that Dickens introduced it into his *Pickwick Papers*, and with it that immortal character, Sam Weller.

The sign of the White Hart carried the badge of Richard II, and this may possibly have influenced Cade's choice, since Richard had been deposed by Henry of Lancaster. However, the greater probability is that it was the inn best fitted to accommodate a man who had ambitions to kingship. It was roomy and for its day large, the most convenient and perhaps the biggest and best-equipped hostelry for Cade and his lieutenants.

Not all Cade's force withdrew with him and the main body. Some contingents remained behind for the express purpose of smelling out the whereabouts of the evil men of the King's Court whom they knew or suspected to be hiding still in London. As earlier stated, however, most of these, with a few important exceptions, had gone into the country. There is no record that at any moment of this or the next day these troops in London went into action, and there is little doubt that they returned eventually to Southwark with news of the whereabouts of those who had rashly or bravely remained within reach.

Night fell, and looking across to the south bank of the river, the apprehensive citizens, to some extent reassured by the discipline of the rebels and the absence of wanton pillage, could see the camp fires, hear the trumpet notes, catch glimpses of movement against the fitful light of torches and even, perhaps, snatches of the songs soldiers tend to sing when their bellies are full and the ale has flowed freely. Though this day had been a parade, a colourful show of the armed might of a velvet-gloved but new and formidable power, there was always tomorrow. Who among them knew what that might bring?

[5]

A CLOSE GUARD had quietly been put by the Mayor upon the approaches to the bridge, and all gates, lanes and steps leading to the river from the London side were covered by armed sentries. It was forbidden to pass weapons out of the city. There were no cannon available in the city to Cade's forces. What there were were in the Tower. Even if Cade had possessed ordnance, he might not have had men trained to aim and fire, and this applies equally to the citizens, had they chosen to defend the Bridge. All they had was a mangonel for hurling stones, but this was placed, quietly again, where it commanded the wharves along the river. To each Alderman four able men were allotted, so that any outbreak of violence in his ward could be quickly dealt with. In this way, the Londoners made ready either to repel, if ordered, a fresh incursion into the city, or to control any drunken, dangerous irregulars who might break camp and cross the bridge on a looting expedition.

The skirts of history can now be lifted for a tantalising moment to give us an authentic glimpse of John Mortimer (Cade) at the White Hart Inn in Southwark. This glimpse is provided by John Payn, a retainer of the knight, Sir John Fastolf, who, in 1465, fifteen years later, was to set down an account of his meeting with the rebel leader in a letter preserved in that wonderful collection known as the Paston Letters.

Payn was older by the time he set down his recollections, and his memory of incidents that had occurred a decade and a half previously may have been defective. They would have been better written down at the time. There is also the suspicion one cannot but feel that the letter itself exaggerated his troubles because its purpose was to cadge money from the person to whom it was sent.

Nevertheless, it is the only first-hand record we have of

Cade as seen by a man who actually met him, and as such, it cannot be ignored. If not pure history, it is the next best thing.

Payn writes that he was ordered by Sir John Fastolf, his employer, to take horse and ride with a companion to Cade for the purpose of obtaining a number of unspecified articles. These may have been copies of the original proclamation for distribution in Fastolf's district, but more probably Payn was sent to spy upon the rebel chief and report on his character and prospects. (It was important to these landed gentry to make certain they did not put their money on the wrong horse.)

After some fruitless riding in search of Cade (see p. 69), Payn caught up with him, and promptly sent his companion and both horses back, no doubt to inform Sir John that he had successfully encountered the rebel force and was about to execute his mission. Not unnaturally he was questioned by the Cade men concerning his reasons for coming to their camp, and replied that he come merely to see his wife's brother and other friends in the rebel army.

He had the misfortune, however, to be recognised by the soldiers as a member of Fastolf's retinue, and was instantly arrested. He was then taken under escort to every part of the camp, preceded by a herald proclaiming him a spy, so that if he had, indeed, a brother-in-law with the rebel army, he could pick him out and prove his good faith. (The herald had been in the service of Henry Holland, Duke of Exeter, and may have been captured at Solefields and forced to serve Cade.)

No such brother-in-law came forward to testify for him, and matters looked grim for the intruder. He was, however, a man of great resource and claimed that if he could be taken to see the Captain and his life were spared, he had 'secret news' to reveal. Cade thereupon saw Payn and told him bluntly that Fastolf, his employer, was one of those he considered primarily to blame for the reduction of the English garrisons in France which had led to their defeat and the loss of valuable French territory. He also asserted that Fastolf was raising an army, which he had quartered at his house in Southwark, and which he proposed to employ in the destruction of the Kentish force.

That Cade said any such thing is doubtful, though a grain or two of fact may lie among the chaff.

Whether or not he believed his own accusations, Cade ordered Payn to be beheaded. At the appointed time, the spy was led from the guard-room or whatever miserable corner of the camp had been his prison, and taken to a patch of grass outside the Captain's tent. The axe and the block, which had already done service, were solemnly brought and set before him. The end of the plausible rascal appeared imminent.

Yet Payn had, after all, made one true statement. He *did* have a brother-in-law in the camp, and one with great influence. This was Robert Poynings. Poynings was the uncle of the Countess of Northumberland. He was married to a member of the Paston family, and his widow, after his death at the second battle of St Albans, was allowed to retain his property. His son became a Lord Deputy of Ireland, and was himself one of those who took up arms against Richard III in 1483, in Kent. This son was the celebrated author of Poynings Law.

Poynings's function was to carry the Captain's naked sword before him on all ceremonial occasions, arrange the places of his guests at table, taste his food to ensure it was good and not poisoned, carve his meat, and act as one of his principal advisers. His high position probably explains why he had not immediately seen and welcomed the miserable man while he was being led about the camp for recognition. It also explains why the rough soldiers did not associate the Poynings with whom Payn claimed kinship with their high officer. Sentries in a British camp would have been most reluctant to go with a spy to Field Marshal Montgomery's aide-de-camp because he said his brother-in-law's name was De Guingand.

Poynings and his friends at once pleaded Payn's cause, and prevailed upon Cade, either by eloquence or by veiled threats, to spare the accused man. Possibly, too, they desired not to fall foul of Fastolf. Cade, though giving way in the end, made a number of conditions. On Payn's release, he was to undertake to return at once to Fastolf's house in Southwark, arm himself as effectively as possible with whatever he found there, rejoin the insurgents, and bring back what news he could of Fastolf's plans.

Payn claims that he did as he was told, but when he reached the house in Southwark, found means of warning his master, the knight, and persuaded him to hide his armour and disband his troop. Sir John had the good sense to act upon this advice – doubtless his servant had reported favourably and accurately upon the efficiency and determination of the rebels – and betook himself with all but two of his men to the shelter of the Tower to save his house from being burned to the ground with everything it contained, which it had been made clear would happen if he did not comply.

Once assured of his master's safety, Payn hastened to obey, nominally, his order from Cade. He bought or appropriated a few small pieces of clothing and enough provisions to meet the needs of his journey, at a cost of about four pounds (six marks.) By this time, however, Cade himself had moved into Southwark. He had evidently not lost sight of the pardoned spy, for according to Payn's own account, he was caught again by the Captain's men and taken to the White Hart, having no doubt been picked up at Fastolf's house before he had got away to rejoin his master. Once again his fate depended on his ingenuity and the whim of the rebel leader.

That Payn had not armed himself, as directed, and that Fastolf had fled to the Tower, evidently infuriated Cade. Looking at the captive, he decided again that he should be stripped and beheaded. Men were sent to search Payn's quarters at Fastolf's house, and returned bringing money, harness, rich robes and clothing. Payn claims in his own defence that this money was merely a sum repaid to him by a priest to whom he had lent it, but in all probability he had been helping himself to the knight's property after his, Fastolf's, departure and had packed these spoils into a chest in readiness either for selling them in the black markets of Southwark, or for his own use.

In the nick of time, Poynings once more interceded with the Captain, and secured Payn's release; but this time Cade was not such a fool as to let him go free. He was allowed to remain in the camp, but was carefully watched, given equipment and arms, and incorporated in the rebel army. If his story is true, he was later to take part in the great battles of July, as shall be told in a later section of this book.

[6]

ON THE MORNING following his first entry into London, Cade once more rode across the undefended, open bridge into the hot, close streets of the city, leaving behind him Southwark with its flat and marshy lands. It was the first Friday in July. Southwark had had many advantages for him as a resting-place. It had not been defended against him because there were few fortifications, but it commanded the main southern approach to the city. Whoever held it virtually denied the use of London Bridge to the loyalists and could hamper the provisioning and trade of her merchants and citizens.

Not only this, but Southwark had a considerable population for the time, whose services were at his disposal for such work as he required. It possessed, in addition to the White Hart, a number of excellent hostelries, one of which was the Tabard Inn made famous by Chaucer in *Canterbury Tales*. His men could find in these refreshment, entertainment and company, over and above the limited facilities of the camp. What is more, the writ of the Londoners did not run here, for the city had no jurisdiction whatsoever over Southwark. All proclamations by her Aldermen and Councillors could, therefore be ignored, and would cause no uneasiness among any who chose to help or shelter the insurgents.

In those days, indeed, this town on the south bank of the Thames was a hive of foreigners, shady characters, the poor, the wretched, the sick, the brothel-keepers and the pimps. Many of these welcomed the arrival of Cade's men for obvious reasons, hoping to profit by it both immediately and in the future.

What picture did London present to the Captain as he rode over the bridge towards her? From the middle of the bridge he could see the wharves on the northern shore at which ships from abroad tied up and discharged. These wharves extended as far as the Tower of London. In the centre was a quay reserved mainly for the wool trade, to which the bales for export were sent. A somewhat larger erection than the rest was the Customs Office. To the east of this, a quay existed predominantly for use by the Italians, whose galleys brought in oil, wine, lace and silks, leather goods and the articles favoured by the English, at least those who could afford them. The French, too, had a favoured wharf for their salt and wines. Their salt trade was particularly important, because in those days the only meat an Englishman could obtain and safely eat during summer and autumn was salt meat. Salt, therefore, was in great demand by the salters.

To the west of the Customs Office there was a series of wharves, smaller in size, named after those who owned them, each serving a specific trade. For example, Asslyn's wharf was used by traders in provisions. Browne's wharf was one of the largest, rivalled only by that of Thomas Bledisloe. These wharves were the centre and focus of the export and import of corn, grain, cloth and other wares. Each of these two wharfowners had built a residence for himself beside the warehouses in which his goods were stored.

Above the bridge was a second string of wharves, also used by the export trade. Not all the vessels plying between Britain and alien lands could berth there. As at Port Swettenham in Malaya today, some ships were too big or could not find room, and consequently these had to load from or discharge into lighters. The river itself was full of barges going up and down on regular journeys, laden with wine, fish, household goods. Some took as much as four days to reach Henley.

Leaving the wharves aside, Cade entered the city of London by way of narrow streets, cobbled, but with no separate sidewalk for pedestrians. Down the centre of each street ran a channel into which rubbish and unwanted liquids were thrown. The streets stinking in the hot sun of July had no dignity. The leader could not have ridden a hundred yards without encountering monks, nuns or friars, who, combined, made up a third of the total population of the city. For this reason, Cade must have made his way past more than one of the religious houses, guilds and brotherhoods which then took up more than a half of the city's area.

The rest of the common people, as distinct from their overlords, were going about their business as usual, whatever the apprehensions they felt as the noise of jingling harness and tramping feet reached them. Among them were labourers, women servants, masons, carpenters, tilers, slaters and their labourers, craftsmen of every kind, not to mention the idlers, the shifty, the criminal, the ostlers and waggoners, the peascod sellers, the vendors of strawberries and cherries, the hawkers of spices, pepper, saffron, cloves, rice, flour and grain. Each, as in an African market today, had his strip of sacking spread out in the shade of the walls, with his wares feebly scattered over it in a primitive display, or walked the streets with a yoke on his shoulders from which baskets hung, or stood, baskets on robust arm, intoning his age-old cry to attract the potential buyer. (It was too early as yet for the pimps, the bawds, the whores.)

One pictures these traders appealing vainly to the marching men, or hastily carrying their perishables out of reach of the hooves of the horses and the stamping feet of the infantrymen, sounding ever closer in the stinking thoroughfare.

At Cheapside, where an open space was occupied by a market, Cade and his men either brushed aside or saw rapidly disappear the stalls carrying fine lawn cloth, cotton goods and thread from Paris, drugs and quack remedies for every ailment. In the region of East Cheap were the vendors of meat and hot pies; the piled pewter pots glittering in the sun, polished as they had been to catch the eye; the stalls from which musical instruments could be bought, such as harps, pipes and psalters. Appendages to this reputable merchandise, but distinctly more plebeian and utilitarian, were the dumps of coal and sand dotted about and well-guarded by the sellers. In the middle of the market place stood the Cross of St Eleanor, and here were the conduits that carried water through the city. It was these very conduits and others less decent that, according to Shakespeare, Cade promised should run with wine.

If he had passed by London Stone again, he would have seen there the drapers, clothiers, sellers of hot sheep's feet, as well as the sellers of rushes, green and sweet-smelling, for the floors of houses. Here, too, were the fishmongers, with mackerel predominating on their moist and slimy stalls.

Cade rode on into Cornhill, where the 'black market' of the city existed, and where the townsfolk could buy what had been burgled the night before or pilfered an hour or two ago from honest citizens. Here, a man whose hood had been snatched from his head in Westminster once came upon it exposed for sale . . .

On he rode into Smithfield or the 'smooth field', where cattle could be bought and a hay market was held, a flat and roomy area which on other days was used for games, tournaments, and – most popular 'show' of all—public executions. The great houses towards which Cade proceeded were built around a central space or courtyard, about 30 ft square. On one side of this was a hall with a main living room facing a garden, designed for both ornaments and the growing of useful vegetables and herbs. The hall itself in these upper-class houses was extensive, with an area of about 40 by 24 ft. Elsewhere there would be other rooms.

A rich merchant such as the detested Philip Malpas would almost certainly have as one of these additional rooms a private chapel for his own use and that of his family. The size of the remaining rooms would be governed by the general area. The garden would not be large by modern standards – probably no more than 70 by 45 ft – unless the house were away from the city proper, when it might well be considerably larger, with even a section given over to the growing of vines for the sake of their grapes.

The courtyard would not be roofed over. The building itself would have a framework of timber with a stone foundation, under which a vault was hollowed out and ran under the main rooms of the house. This was used for storing all the merchant's goods and treasures.

Facing the street there was a gatehouse, or what today would be called the gatekeeper's lodge, and on each side of this would be either the domestic offices or subsidiary small houses in which servants were housed.

On the other hand, ordinary shopkeepers were housed far less luxuriously. Their dwellings consisted of a shop, a kitchen, and beneath these, a cellar. The shop had a counter, and round its walls ran some form of display advertisement, probably a piece of black buckram on which a flowery picture had been painted by an itinerant sign-writer or by the shop-keeper himself. The goods for sale would be set out on stalls in the front, and there would be a stock room next to the shop with additional counters. In this type of dwelling the hall was used as the living-room (as in the lounge-halls so familiar in modern comedies). The ceiling of this was of deal imported from the Baltic countries.

Beyond the hall was the kitchen, stone-flagged and provided with a leaden cistern, a 'dressing board', a pair of shelves and a hatch. There would also be a pantry in which butter and cream were made and stored. By law, a lantern had to be hung outside each dwelling. Upstairs were three rooms for sleeping, with one bed always made up. Of these, one would contain a press or wardrobe with boards round it and closed underneath.

A frontage of fifty yards might contain no fewer than twelve houses in a district such as Charing Cross. There would, of course, be a large proportion of hovels for the poor, much smaller and of mean appearance and interior.

[7]

THE MOOD in which Cade re-entered London on this, the second, day of his triumph was different from that of the previous day. Then he had presented himself to the populace as potentially regal, a reassuring, courteous, colourful presence, suggesting an able warrior in full control of his men. Now his tactics changed. Some subtle infiltration of the poison of absolute power had entered his veins, or pressure had been brought to bear upon him in his own council chamber. He was determined now to wreak a foretaste of popular vengeance upon those guilty men his spies had revealed as accessible to him. He may have been convinced by persuasion concealing menace that he could not retain control of the men under him unless he showed clearly that he could be both brutal and swift. The Kentish men had not come to London to march through crowded streets and do nothing.

Men are quick to impute treachery or corruption to a leader who, once he has achieved power, fails to punish or destroy his open enemies. His mission now, whatever had inspired it, was essentially one of chastisement.

One of the less trustworthy chroniclers, writing decades later, declares that Cade dined at the house of, and presumably with, Philip Malpas in St Margaret Pattens (a church embodied in the parish of St Saviour's at the break-up of the monasteries), and robbed him before taking his leave.

That Cade should have dined with one who was a particular favourite of the Court party is so unlikely that it must be regarded as a fabrication. It is as if Zhukov, having captured Berlin, should have accepted an invitation to dine in their bunker with Goebbels or Speer, and that having accepted the invitation, he should after the meal have robbed his host. Cade never at any time indulged in petty thievery. He had claimed to be a 'gentleman', and this claim had to be supported by his conduct. Even in those days the last thing he would do would be to abuse hospitality in so cheap and sordid a manner.

What happened is that the rebel chief descended upon Malpas as the culprit most easily reached, and finding him gone, as he must have done, proceeded to put his mansion to the sack. Silver and gold, merchandise such as tin, wood, madder, alum, woollen cloth, jewels, feather bedding, napery, tapestries, all these were looted either by Cade and his men, or by the mob ever at his heels when plunder lay in the offing. Malpas was punished after this fashion because known to be one of the Court favourites, and an evil influence in the Council of the city. Possibly his flight followed another of the secret warnings of the underhand and ubiquitous Cooke, who was later, as has been pointed out, to become his son-in-law.

One proof, however, exists that certain of his possessions did fall into Cade's keeping. In his house the merchant kept a number of jewels belonging to the Duke of York. These had been entrusted to him either for safe keeping, as today one sends treasured possessions to one's Bank for safe deposit, or as a pledge for a badly-needed loan. These were among the items confiscated by the Captain of Kent, and later recovered, and this is one of the arguments tending to prove that the

Duke of York himself cannot have had personal dealings with or supported the rebel leader.

That the sacking of the Malpas residence occurred on the day after Cade's first entry into the city cannot be satisfactorily established. Some of the chronicles are vague on the point. It is improbable, however, that the action took place during the first triumphal entry, with its tact and caution, its obvious desire to eliminate whatever of fear and doubt lingered in the minds of the Londoners, and when Cade himself was still uncertain of his reception.

By the following day, however, his mastery of the city had been effectively demonstrated, he had proclaimed his lordship at the Stone, and now the time had come to bring justice to the guilty. His tactics accordingly changed. There is, indeed, only one genuine argument to suggest that the Malpas raid took place on the first day: that after the dramatic incident at London Stone there is no explicit account of what Cade did with the rest of that day. As has been suggested in the previous pages, however, it was probably spent in taking over the city in detail and preparing for the cruel and tragic events of the following day.

Whatever Cade did during the rest of Friday, 3rd July, at its close he once again returned to his lodging in Southwark to spend there yet another night, a night pregnant with terrible decisions, made either by the leader in communion with himself during the small hours, or in conclave with his followers. There is a record that many of the simple common folk of London made their way over London Bridge to the White Hart Inn that night hoping to be given jobs under the new régime. Some of them stayed there all night. With them went *agents provocateurs* to take advantage of their simplicity, foment anger at their failure to win an audience from the Captain, and turn them by dawn into a violent and reckless mob. Their aim was to discredit the rebels, cause the first natural popularity of their chief to wane and ultimately die.

So, once again, the heavy weight of a new hand lifts from

Wat Tyler is stabbed by Sir William Walworth, Lord Mayor of London

Richard II appeases the rebels on the death of Tyler

the city for a few dark hours. London sleeps more easily. No citizen has had his throat cut. No innocent woman has been molested. No house is in flames, and the goods of the merchants lie still undisturbed in their cellars. Malpas has been pillaged, it is true, but – as the saying goes in such hours when uneasy men seek to minimise their danger – 'he deserved it'. There is no inkling of the blood that is to flow before nightfall next day.

SEVEN

The Day of Executions

[1]

SATURDAY saw Cade once more advance in force across London Bridge. This time there was no softness of mood, no flattering smiles for the mob, no harangues from the street corners, no pretence of gentle, undemanding occupation. The armour, the helmets, the swords, glittered in the morning sun; the cloaks, swaying, stained the day with bright colours; the faces of the leading ranks were unchanged; outwardly it was as before; but there was a difference. The city had admitted not a suppliant, but a master, about to show his mastery. The time had come for those who skulked in the shadows, hoping against hope they would be left untouched, to be dragged from their miserable refuges and made to feel the hatred their deeds had won for them in the hearts of humble men.

Of these guilty personages, the three most important were Sir James Fiennes, Lord Saye and Sele, Speaker in Suffolk's Parliament of 1449; Lord Treasurer of England; owner by royal decree of a rich mansion at Witley in Surrey, as well as the great house at Knole. Saye was believed to have been bribed to sell the Dukedom of Maine to the French.

Saye's title had been recently acquired from John de Clinton, a Sussex kinsman. (His brother, Sir Roger Fiennes, who built the castle at Herstmonceaux, was equally unpopular, so that some of those nearest to him provided the greater part of Cade's following in Sussex.)

The other two were William Crowmer and Bishop Waynflete.

Crowmer was Sheriff of Kent in the Easter term of 1450, having succeeded Stephen Slegg. He held the manor of Tunstall in Kent, and was both an Esquire and the son-in-law of Saye. His iron heel on their necks had been most cruelly felt and savagely resented by the rebels from Kent. Slegg, his predecessor, was another of those named by Cade as a tax extortioner, and with him were coupled William Isle, twice the county's representative, and Robert Est.

Waynflete we shall meet again.

It has been indicated that Saye was sheltering in the Tower together with the Archbishops of Canterbury and York, under the Governor's protection. Waynflete, however, had flown to a Priory in Holywell, where was a mineral spring of some sanctity. (This spring was popular down to the Reformation, but was filled in after it as encouraging superstition. A hundred years later Sadler rediscovered it, and thus gave his name to Sadlers Wells.)

Crowmer was in the Fleet prison, and being the easiest to capture, was the first to suffer. Cade's first call, however, was at Newgate, where he released a large number of political and other prisoners. Crowmer was then dragged from his cell and carried to Mile End, where contact had evidently been made with the men of Essex encamped in the fields there. With no more than a summary trial he was beheaded in a field beyond Aldgate 'beside Clopton ys Place'. Also beheaded at the same time, at Whitechapel, probably by his own companions, was a Colchester man named Baylly (Bailey), who claimed that he knew Cade, and assured his hearers that the Captain was a man of lowly birth. When consulted by the Essex leaders, Cade denied all personal knowledge of the man and declared him to be a necromancer of evil repute and character whose 'books' would prove this accusation. Bailey was searched, and the 'books' discovered, concealed on his person. Calumniators assert that Cade repudiated Bailey because he knew too much about him, but no evidence is brought to support this contention.

It is strange that the trouble should have been taken to transport Crowmer all the way to Mile End and try him in the presence of the army from Essex. The explanation may well be that not only was this a good moment in which to link up with these allies, but also it was a means of demonstrating to them, stuck at Mile End as they were, that Cade had London at his feet, could not only open her prisons (and by implication close them upon the recalcitrant or disloyal), but was also fully prepared and able to avenge the sufferings of England upon those responsible for them. He may have wished to encourage these laggards or at least stimulate them into activity.

While these events were taking place, a different and equally sombre scene was being enacted outside the Tower of London.

[2]

HAVING DISPOSED OF CROWMER, on his way under guard to Mile End, Cade now appeared in force at the gates of the Tower, demanding that Lord Saye be handed over to him for judgement. Lord Scales, the Governor, was in a difficult position. He had a few guns, but no great number. His instructions from the King had been to 'defend' the fortress, not to sally forth from it. The loyalty of his troops was probably doubtful. Almost certainly some of those back from the French wars resented having been prevented from re- turning at once to their homes. If, therefore, Cade were to attack in force, it was quite on the cards that the Tower would fall.

Not only this, but in his heart, perhaps, Scales had some sympathy with the rebels. An honest soldier, he could not but feel that Saye, an unwanted guest, had earned the punishment that was about to be administered. His patriotic sentiments must have been outraged by the surrender of Maine and Anjou.

It is doubtful also whether Scales grasped that execution inevitably awaited his prisoner. Not yet knowing of the approaching death of Crowmer, he may well have refused to consider the possibility that Cade would dare to inflict upon so high a dignitary more than a heavy fine or at the worst, a beating. Saye might in the end be held as a hostage.

The value of the Tower to the royal cause, and of his men's lives to their commander, themselves, and their fortress, may have seemed to him to outweigh his responsibility for the goods and freedom of an obvious rascal – for had not the King himself sent Saye to the Tower? (Military men have never loved politicians). When Cade's envoy presented himself, therefore, and there had been time to consider his message, Scales quickly decided that the safest plan was to give up the wanted courtier, on condition, however, that Cade undertook not to attack the Tower, nor to interfere with its Governor in the execution of his proper duties as its Keeper. To this condition Cade agreed.

So, in a short time, the gates opened to allow guards – ready for any sign of treacherous entry – to lead out and deliver to the waiting insurgents a pathetic, shrunken figure, that of their oppressor. It is difficult to believe that Saye knew what lay in store for him. Men who have exercised great power without hindrance find it impossible to believe that once the hypnotic influence of their high office has been dissipated by events, they are no more to their enemies than any other bundle of flesh and nerves capable of feeling pain, as easy to decapitate as the humblest country chicken. They advance towards captivity unknowing that that poor body of theirs, before which men have bowed down, to whose slightest gesture deference has been paid, is as negligible now as the calf to the slaughterman. They go to their deaths believing that power is an objective reality, intimately bound up with their own being; something that must, like an aura, surround them, preventing gross misuse of their persons. It is inalienably theirs, aweful, terrible, and recognised as such by all beneath them.

In this belief, perhaps, Saye went forward towards his captors, erect, unflinching, unashamed. Power, inseparable from his person, must, he thought, exert its influence and preserve him from rough contact as a magnet may, properly held, repel as well as attract.

He was wrong.

[3]

IT IS SOME PROOF of the Captain of Kent's wish to observe the decencies that he did not kill Saye out of hand, but had him brought to the Guildhall (Yelde Hall), so that he might be given a formal trial with all the proper observances. He was to be examined there by those justices sitting at the time. Saye is said to have refused to plead and to have insisted to the Lord Mayor that he be tried by his peers, but this plea was refused. (It is doubtful, indeed, if enough of his peers remained in London to make up a sufficient body.) Among his many other crimes he was accused of causing the death of the Duke of Gloucester, but only one of the Chronicles suggests that he confessed to this.

This Duke, fourth son of Henry IV, was fifty-six at the time of his death in 1447. He had fought at Agincourt as a young man, and had been Regent of England in 1421 and 1422. He was a man of turbulent character, ambitious, ever intriguing, and perpetually a thorn in the side of the abler, more mature men who had the task of governing England for the King. In 1441, his wife had been accused of practising sorcery against him and condemned. He had tried to prevent the King's marriage to Margaret of Anjou, which brought him into conflict with the Duke of Suffolk. When Parliament met at Bury St Edmunds in 1447, Humphrey was immediately arrested on his arrival there, and died in captivity four days later.

It was always believed that his death was the result of Suffolk's hatred for him, and Saye was regarded as the man who had carried out the command to dispose of him. A cultured man, fond of reading and a patron of scholars, the Duke was popular with the commonalty, but that he died at the hands of an assassin is improbable. He had lived a dissipated life, had undergone privations and stress in war, and had for many years been eaten up by jealousy and frustration. Reading of his career, one cannot but see in his behaviour every indication that he was a cancer subject, and this disease was probably the cause of his death.

Justice even in the fifteenth century had its own momentum, which it was difficult to accelerate. The pace was not swift enough for the hotter heads among the Kentish men. Like all practitioners of lynch law, they wanted revenge and wanted it quickly. As the day drew to its close, and there was still no sign that the justices had decided the case, they burst into the chamber where the trial was proceeding. Ignoring remonstrances, they thrust aside the few who tried to hinder them, tore the defendant from the dock, and dragged him as they had dragged Crowmer, not this time to Mile End, but to Smithfield, where they beheaded him after insult, blows and humiliation. The place of execution in this instance was the Standard at Cheapside, nearly opposite Bow Churchyard and the scene of many earlier executions. The Standard was a conduit so old that it had become extremely dilapidated, but it was later reconstructed in stone by Thomas Knolles. William of Worcester, the most accurate of all the chroniclers, gives the time of Saye's death as seven in the evening. He was not 'shriven' before he died, and this probably shocked decent Londoners even more than the summary beheading of their former Lord Treasurer.

The standards of the fifteenth century were, it was once believed, incredibly low as compared to those of today. It has taken Auschwitz and Belsen, the Siamese railway, the prison camps of Siberia, the cruelties of the Congo, to reveal that there is still a dark reservoir of hate and ferocity in Man which bursts through whenever there appears a weakness in the imprisoning crust of courtesy and tolerance, of order and goodwill. Whether Cade ordered these executions and what followed them, or, as is possible, his men acted on their own initiative, it is true that there now took place, after two savage, but perhaps excusable, murders, a vulgar obscene maltreatment of the dead bodies. It is written down that Saye's severed head, with Crowmer's, were placed lip-to-lip in a ghastly kiss, and the naked bodies drawn at the tails of horses so roughly that their flesh adhered to the stones. From the Standard in Cheapside, over London Bridge, and so to St Thomas Watring in Southwark, these trailing rags of white flesh, spattered and streaming with blood, were dragged.

There they were hung, Saye's body being 'drawn and quartered' to use the archaic phrase, and both heads, having been carried on long poles, set up on the Bridge itself. The heads of two common malefactors already there were taken down to make room for them.

One of the prisoners in Newgate when Cade made his appearance there had been that selfsame Robert Horne who had been imprisoned for urging resistance to the rebels. Cade could have executed this man, too, but demanded of him instead the sum of approximately £170 as a fine. This sum Horne paid, and was accordingly released, after which he was not further harmed or interfered with. Cade could be harsh with the royal favourites and dignitaries, but was too big a man to conduct a purely personal vendetta against one who had done no more than honestly speak his mind. Moreover, he was approached by both Horne's wife and his friends, who pleaded with him to spare the unfortunate Alderman. As we have seen with Payn, Cade was susceptible to personal appeals. There are men who find clemency an agreeable exercise of power. Cade was one of them.

[4]

IT WAS EVENING by the time these deeds, eventually so fatal to Cade's ambitions, were done, and the need of refreshment made the new lord of London ride to the region of Tower Street in the parish of St Margaret Pattens. Here he sought out a citizen whose name is variously given as Ghirstes, Girste or Cherstis, and who was high on the list of those with whom scores had to be settled. (The modern version would be 'Curtis'.) This time it was not blood but cash – with which to buy provisions and supplies for his men – that was required. Faced with unpleasant possibilities if he refused, Curtis paid up, seething, though he concealed his rage. The mob is said to have aided Cade in this deed.

(Some scepticism exists regarding this story. Possibly this was one of those acts attributed to Cade, but in reality committed by some unscrupulous members of his troop.)

From Cade's point of view it had been, despite its atrocities, a good day. Justice had been done to the tyrants, even if the manner of it had been swift and ferocious. Money, badly needed, had been successfully extorted from the enemy. A working agreement had been made with the Governor of the Tower; and a solemn warning of what the 'traitors' on his list might expect was visible, bloody and foul, on London Bridge. Contact had been made with the Essex force. There had been no open opposition in the city. The one uneasiness was the stinking mob of pickers and stealers who followed him wherever he went, the spawn of the slums of London, wanting only half a chance to burgle, kill, and burn.

The time had now come to return to Southwark. The leader gave the appropriate order, and the force – numerous and well-equipped, or Lord Scales would not so readily have

surrendered his prisoner – made their way jubilantly back
over the bridge, grinning at the severed heads past which they
rode, and being grinned at horribly in return. Singing,
content, they moved towards their quarters as the light faded
and the torches and lanterns of the encampment shone out a
welcome.

One last grim decision had, however, to be made before
Cade could repair to the White Hart and take his ease. A
thief named William Haywardyn, of the parish of St Martin
in London, caught in the act of stealing, was brought before
him. Without hesitation, Cade ordered him to be beheaded.
The sentence was promptly carried out as a warning to the
rabble whom success had brought to Southwark, and whom
Cade had observed and despised.

[5]

NIGHTFALL did not put an end to the activities of London's
citizens. Under cover of darkness, the scum poured out of
their alleys, from under arches, from cellar and hovel, and the
moment Cade's men had departed and all that could be seen
were the gently swinging house-lanterns and the occasional
torch, their work began. Looting, pillaging, arson, even
murder, perhaps, were accompanied by rape and mutilation.
The narrow ways were aquiver with strangulated cries, with
the rush of sparks and flame, the hiss and mutter of urgent
conspirators. Screams tore the silence into tatters. There
were sounds of running feet, howls of a greedy mob bent on
destruction, the thuds of heavy battering rams on the doors of
merchants' houses either empty or refusing to open, the
shouts of elation as men ran out clutching treasures in their
arms. Quarrels among the looters were arrested by the quick
thrust of a blade and the noise of a heavy fall. It was a
medieval 'night of the long knives'.

Years later, and even the next day, all this was ascribed

to the Kentish men. There were many whose interest it was to have this believed and spread around. There may even have been, as on the night before, some instigation and encouragement by those whose profit was not immediate, but might be great in the future.

Gradually, too, there spread from mouth to mouth rumours of decisions the rebel leader had taken. He was said to have created Aldermen such men as a rich drysalter named Stoke-woode, who had informed upon those of his neighbours hostile to the insurrection. It was said that these men had his sanction to blackmail any who could be accused, with some show of reason, of having been lukewarm to his coming, of having actively attacked him in conversation, or of deserving to die. The wife of a man who had been ordered to patrol the river before Cade arrived, to prevent him from crossing it, was mentioned as having had to pay lest he should be betrayed.

The wealthy men who ran the city had no feeling of sympathy for the oppressed commoners. The rights and wrong of the revolt entered hardly at all into their calculations, and the discovery that men had died of hunger owing to the mismanagement and selfishness of so-called statesmen made no impression on them. They were having no 'Charter of Liberties' thrust upon them if they could help it. All they cared for, outside their own private domestic attachments, were their money-bags and possessions, the safety of their property. Terrified by the exaggerated reports of sack and destruction by bands of ruffians pretending to belong to the camp across the water, they conferred in haste to see what could be done.

From the country, messengers came to them secretly telling of so-called 'captains' plundering the priesthood and the wealthy in Cade's name, though entirely without his knowledge. What they conveniently ignored was that in fact the plundered had been robbed by the very men against whom Cade had risen. They merely transferred the crimes of the guilty to their victims. For example, the Chancery records speak of a Suffolk squire who evicted a man from the lands he coveted. One and all in the city now feared anarchy.

Hitherto Cade had been largely sustained by the money received from his supporters; but these men also had been frightened by what they saw or imagined. Money was Cade's lifeline, as it is of any rebel force, and the plotters perceived that by a little agreement among themselves and a well-thought-out plan, they could sever it.

There was much going to and fro, much quiet preparation, much secret whispering and careful movement of materials, but there was one terrible obstacle – lack of time. Cade would be back in the city once more next morning, and this time many heads might roll and the brains of loyalist captains be beaten out before they had achieved their ends. Time was what they needed and prayed for; time, time, time!

Time, too, was the one commodity that Cade, if he sought to remain lord of London, and still more if he truly wished, as Shakespeare believed he did, to become King of England, could now not afford to give them. Every man of intelligence in the city knew this and cursed the hours as they went by all too quickly.

And meanwhile Cade was sleeping quietly at the White Hart Inn, and Thames was rolling rapidly.

EIGHT

Quiet Sunday

[1]

A MAN WHO SEEKS supreme power must be ruthless and swift in decision when his power or his interests are threatened. He must make time serve him while he has it, and use it as what it is, the sharpest weapon in his armoury. As a tactician Cade was competent. As a statesman he had qualities that might have burgeoned and flowered after he had occupied the seat of power. As a strategist, however, he was weak, and it was this weakness that lost him a throne.

It has been seen that instead of taking London by the throat while she lay at his mercy after the victory of Sevenoaks, he dawdled and hesitated like a footballer fearing to shoot for goal. Fate, or whatever it may be called, allowed him to waste this opportunity, and as is her way, offered him a second chance to prove himself. He wasted this, too.

Looking over the slender sheaf of hard fact available to the historian after five hundred odd years, it seems clear that Cade's greatest blunder was the failure to storm and capture the Tower of London. He had had it virtually in his grasp the previous day, but he chose instead, either from temerity or because he was in too big a hurry to execute Saye, to be content with a truce. By the night of Sunday it was too late. Thirty-six hours had elapsed, thirty-six hours that could never be recovered.

It is authoritatively recorded that all day Sunday, the day following his executions, he remained quiescent in Southwark. Neither he nor his army moved. The respite, the time, given to his enemies in the city was magnificently used, and luck, which had been his, now deserted him.

Had he captured and held the Tower, resistance in London would have been impracticable. There would have been no citadel acting as focus and bulwark, no hostile guns, no military ability of professional type, behind the disgruntled Londoners. The weak and timorous King had no eloquence capable of rousing a population, no magic to inspire. His queen was everywhere disliked and distrusted, even by the Lancastrians. Cade could have been lord of London in very truth, and to his standard would then have flocked the thousands who had waited to be sure before committing themselves. Having taken full control of the capital, he could and would in all probability have taken the crown.

It was one of those opportunities that seldom come twice. Having taken it, he would have been in reality what he was in appearance. Assault on a strong and well-defended fortress with levies not highly trained for the purpose is always a risk, but it was one he should and could have run. Instead, he made a present to his opponents of the short space of time given to him.

It was all the more an error because it meant that he had to maintain his camp over in Southwark, across the river and right away from the capital itself. Had the Tower been his, he could have made it his headquarters and quartered his troops in the city and its surroundings, where they would have been at hand to quell any disturbances or to prevent the secret movements whose object was soon to be revealed.

It is another of those mysteries that make Cade so interesting a figure that not only should he have lost the fruits of victory by this bad judgement, but that he should also have let an entire critical day go by while he lingered idly at the White Hart. Yet there is a possible and convincing explanation, better than the crude and easy ones that have sometimes been put forward. It has been suggested that the leader, over-confident and drunk with success, gave way to the lusts of the flesh – ate, drank, made free with the wenches at the tavern; or even with the hostess herself, who was to make so gruesome an entrance at a later date.

Another theory is that worn out, perhaps, by his exertions, he made up for loss of sleep by spending long hours in bed. Or there may have been once more dissension in his councils preventing immediate action. The point, however, is that a man who has it in mind to make a bid for the throne of England must not so readily show himself a prey to human weakness, must not lack drive and energy at the one moment that is critical. After the prize has been won, yes. Then the enthroned ruler may relax awhile. But until the prize is his, he dare not linger. It is difficult to believe that Cade was such a fool as these explanations would have us believe.

[2]

NEVERTHELESS, the fact remains that Cade did *not* move. If the reasons suggested do not satisfy, then some other must be advanced that is equally plausible, yet more consistent with the character and ambitions of the man as he has shown himself. The one solution of the problem that has in it an element of truth is that Cade was responsive to the religious beliefs of his period. Prominent among his supporters were men of the church from both Kent and Sussex, and it is likely that these were devout, obedient servants of the Lord. Otherwise they would not have been so greatly moved by the sufferings of their flock as to give their blessing to Cade's men and rise with them. Cade himself – and we know nothing to the contrary – may have been a sincere and earnest member of the Church of Rome. His troops, being countrymen, would have the simple, uncritical faith of their forefathers. In fact, it is said in one account that Cade celebrated High Mass in the camp that Sunday morning, which in itself would account for some hours of military immobility.

But apart from all other considerations, this *was* a Sunday. The distinction between religion and ordinary existence was less sharp then than it has since become. It was the common desire of those who joined in any association such as an army to feel that their actions had spiritual sanction, and to receive from their pastors the blessings and comfort so necessary to them. For all but the wicked and the loose-living, Sunday was no day for war. It was a day of rest. In fact, punishment was recognised as being the just due of those who did not observe the Lord's Day. Lyndwood, a canonist of the century, wrote : 'Canon Law tells us that we must do nothing on the Lord's Day except to spend our time on God. No work is done on that holy day, but it is spent exclusively in hymns and psalms and spiritual songs.'

Dr Coulton records of the fifteenth century that 'works which primarily benefit the body, as distinct from . . . pious and intellectual work' must be abstained from. 'Thus field-work is explicitly forbidden, and markets, and pleas in court except in cases of necessity. In Lynwood's judgement "The man who doth such work sinneth mortally, if by reason of such work he knowingly omits that which pertaineth to God's worship, and whereunto he is bound".'

Sunday was, then, a day of rest, of worship, of quiet self-communion, of confession and absolution, of prayer and spiritual refreshment. To the plain men of Kent, Sussex, and, perhaps, Essex as well, as to their pastors, it was to be spent reverently and in tranquillity. Blood could flow again, fat citizens be 'squeezed', on Monday, but not on the day the Lord had set aside as His own.

It may be argued that little notice is taken of Sundays when men are at war, but in fact Cade was not at the moment at war. The loyal forces were far away in the Midlands. There was an arrangement with the Tower. The city was cowed. All was outwardly quiet. There seemed no reason why the day should not pass peacefully and well.

It is stated that after he had celebrated Mass, Cade executed Thomas Mayne, and an esquire named Hampton, whose crime is not specified. This has been taken to mean that there was trouble in Cade's camp, which held up military action, but the suggestion does not hold water. Any trouble there may have been was over and done with or the execution would never have taken place; Cade could have marched that day had it been his wish or intention. The whole afternoon and evening lay at his disposal. He had eliminated the ringleader of any hostile body and was once more in undisputed command. If he meant to move, there was nothing to stop him.

One is compelled to believe that not this arrested him nor the suspicion that forces were coming into or out of London to oppose him. Nor did he now fear the narrow streets in which it would have been difficult to deploy his men and maintain order of battle. No, Sunday was Sunday. His men knew it. He knew it himself. He saw no reason, had no wish, to break the Sabbath.

Nevertheless, however laudable may have been this decision to be indecisive, it must be regarded as one of the subsidiary causes for the failure of the revolt. Cade's capture of London, like Hitler's of France, had, in fact, come too quickly. It had taken him by surprise and he had no plans worked out to cope with it. The consequence was that he neither effectively occupied the city nor made himself personally responsible for the maintenance of daily or nocturnal order within her boundaries. He had no organisation ready to take over London, district by district, and was compelled to put his trust in the very men who ultimately betrayed him. He seems to have had no notion of how he was going to secure the rest of the country, nor of how to organise a working government. He was a soldier, and rarely in history have soldiers proved efficient national administrators.

H

His decision to become Dictator, if not King, may, more-over, have been secret, limiting his power in council, robbing his words of force. Many of the insurgents would beyond question have rested content with vengeance on the Courtiers and a promise of reform from the King. His present supremacy was the result in their eyes rather of the cowardice and poor judgement of the King and his advisers than of his own military genius or the permanent strength of the rising. The statecraft of his lieutenants is questionable.

If he had had such a plan as the circumstances required, his actions during those few days of absolute power would have been less spasmodic, better-timed, more consistent and effective. One can imagine a clean-cut schedule: (D.1) Enter London; (D.2) Capture Tower of London and arrest Lord Saye; (D.3) Dispose troops in London and take over entire city, arranging for preservation of order and continuance of normal activities; (D.4) Disarm all opposition and issue proclamations covering the next few weeks; (D.5) Prepare plans for defeat of King's army and for the assumption of power throughout England; (D.6) Try and execute if found guilty the captive oppressors and confiscate the estates of those who refuse to give themselves up for trial; (D.7) Advance northwards to meet the King, either in battle or in conference; (D.8) Draw up a new Constitution, if considered necessary after defeat or surrender of King.

No such orderly, systematic plan existed, however. As night fell, Cade remained at the inn in Southwark. His guards patrolling the camp murmured a few words to each other as they met, and reported 'All's well' as they made their rounds. A hush descended on the city.

[3]

THE MEN who ran London, however, valued their safety more than their Sabbath. Seeing no sign of the insurgents as the morning hours dragged by, they took full advantage of their unexpected freedom of action. Their plans complete, the Lord Mayor, Sir Thomas Charlton; Philip Malpas, the pillaged and hunted draper; the Aldermen and Councillors; set off for the Tower, where they sought audience of the Governor. Scales, a loyal servant of the King, was only too glad to find a resurgence of 'guts' among the previously supine and even treacherous worthies of the city. He had welcomed a few days earlier a good officer back from Normandy, a Welshman named Matthew Gough, whom he had recruited for the royal forces as ordered by Henry when he abandoned his city. He now recommended to the Londoners that the entire anti-Cade force, made up of soldiers from the Tower, armed citizens, and any others able and willing to bear arms in defence of their homes, should place themselves under Gough's command. Naturally, Scales could not release the entire garrison of the Tower, but he undertook to support any military operations in which they might be engaged by a bombardment with his guns.

A company of royal archers still quartered in Fleet Street were incorporated in the scratch force, and the entire body quietly assembled under cover of darkness, received their instructions, met their officers, and rehearsed their operations inside the walls of the Tower. In this way Cade's spies in London were prevented from discovering the imminence of attack, while neither the ordinary men and women in the streets nor the watchers on the southern bank of the River at Southwark were made curious or alarmed.

Alderman Robert Horne, the released prisoner, was put in charge of the river. Malpas received command of a detachment under Gough. Some chronicles state that Scales himself took overall command of the battle, but this is questionable. His responsibility was more likely for the general plan of campaign, the execution of which was entrusted solely to Matthew Gough.

Silently, at eight o'clock on that Sunday evening, company

by company, treading softly in the murk of the high-walled narrow streets, empty for the most part because men were reposing in their own homes, the troops filed out of the Tower gates and made their way towards the river. Any rioters they encountered were dispersed and roughly cleared from the streets. Casual passers-by took them, no doubt, for part of Cade's force patrolling for reasons of security, and turned away as quickly as they could.

Once within sight of the bridge, the soldiers took up positions in readiness for the first part of the operation, the capture of London Bridge from the rebels. One pictures them waiting tensely as the last lights go out one by one on the opposite shore, and the still, watered darkness coagulates and thickens, till all that surrounds them is a grey moving ribbon, the Thames; the faint outline, like a black bar across dark silk, of the bridge; and the few winking, glimmering lights that still remain where Cade and his men lie at ease across the river.

It had been a quiet Sunday.

NINE

The Battle of the Bridge

[1]

THE BATTLE FOR LONDON and all that went with it began at nine in the evening. Its essence was a surprise attack. As far as can be judged from the accounts available, the original objective was a strictly limited one, namely, to seize the bridge and deny Cade his only means of ready communication with the city and his supporters there. He would thus be prevented from carrying out further depredations and executing other personages, while at the same time the royal forces assumed to be mustering in the country would be given more time for assembly and advance.

Just as Cade had neglected to prepare detailed plans for the occupation of London and procedure thereafter, so no plans appear to have been drawn up by the Londoners for exploitation of their victory if they should succeed, and if their success should prove to be more complete than they anticipated. Had such plans existed, the results achieved might have constituted a brilliant military triumph ending in complete and final disaster for the rebel army, because the first objectives were, as planned, achieved with comparative ease. The insurgents were taken by surprise. Their sentries were killed, the bridge overrun, and although the troops at the Southwark end fought fiercely, they were mastered and had to retreat almost to the shore.

The mixed army of professional fighting men and citizens had, it seemed, only to pursue them vigorously and with clear purpose to win their way into the Kentish camp. A final thrust at the confused and momentarily disconcerted rebel army might then have sent Cade flying back to the lanes and woods from which he had come. But Gough, either from lack of instructions or because of excessive caution, failed to follow up his swift success. He paused at the Southwark 'stulpes' or piles, holding on meantime to what he had won, clearing away the dead, and sending back the wounded and prisoners, intending to wait either for orders from the Tower, or for daylight to return, when his force could be strengthened from the Tower and march on the enemy camp.

By the standards of the better-known battles of history, that of this July night in 1450 is sensational in neither its strategy nor its tactics. Yet it was as desperate, as bloody, as momentous in its results, as others of greater fame. It brought into opposition two masters of military tactics, both experienced in the arts of war, both representing two eternal adversaries. On the one hand was Cade, fighting, nominally at least, for justice and a better England, for change and reform and a social upheaval. On the other stood Gough, representing loyalty to the King, authority, the established order. Among the humbler combatants, too, noble motives mingled with the instinct for self-preservation and personal ambition. Duty to the regiment and the commander, hatred of tyranny, an instinct to obey, faith and idealism and a yearning to deliver the land from evil, were as much mainsprings of the battle as vengefulness, greed, terror or envy. Motives were never more mixed than on that night, when the sentries Cade had posted on the bridge were suddenly trampled down and a surge of armed men rushed across to break the frail link between the Captain of Kent and his city.

Cade was as good a soldier as, if not better than, Gough. He had not sought a fight, but as the London men had chosen to break the peace, he was not going to leave them unpunished.

By his decision to await the dawn before resuming the contest, Gough had thrown away his tactical advantage. The rebels had been given time to recover. Those sleeping or carousing armed themselves. The first wild onslaught had carried the Londoners as far as what was termed the 'bulwark' of the bridge, where the wooden piles of its foot rested on the Southwark shore. Cade's sentries had been overrun much sooner than he expected, and he himself taken by surprise, but he was not so bad a general as to have taken no precautions against just such an event. Just at the right moment, therefore, when the impetus of Gough's attack had exhausted itself and he was firmly clinging to the bridge he had almost won, Cade threw in a mass of armed men.

The over-confident Londoners were suddenly assailed in turn by strong, skilled, well-armed soldiers, and compelled to defend themselves or be driven back to their starting point and beyond.

[2]

IN THE HEAT of battle, orders do not always reach those for whom they are intended, or do not reach them in time, or are misinterpreted or ignored, or found incapable of execution in the circumstances of the moment. Fighting on a narrow, wooden bridge, with timber houses on each side, in darkness illuminated only by such light as the heavens, a few hanging lamps and the smoking torches of the soldiers, provided, cannot have had the ordered quality of a set battle. Moreover, the combatants were of the same race. Orders shouted in the dark by English voices could be traps for the unwary, especially if commanding retreat.

The chronicles agree that this was one of the bitterest and cruellest conflicts of the age, and all the more so because, in defiance of their religious convictions, Cade and his men had been forced to do battle on the Lord's Day, which they were

physically and mentally disposed to respect. Their hatred of
the opposing faction was stimulated by this direct proof of
irreverence, sacrilege, a ruthless disregard of God's
ordinances. They were inspired now by the belief that the
Lord God would, must, be on their side. Their anger was
greater, their wills fiercer, than they might have been had a
secular day been chosen for the clash.

The struggle that followed was fanatical and passionate.
The close confinement enforced upon the men-at-arms by the
narrowness of the bridge made it a fight of hand-to-hand
character. Cade's onrush gained a little ground, whereupon
Gough threw in reinforcements piecemeal, always bad tactics.
There was no question of manoeuvre. It was will against will,
body against body, and it is doubtful if even the coward or
the wounded could have avoided combat, so close was the
enemy upon him. There are convincing accounts of men
grappling in each other's arms, gripping one another about
the body, striving each to heave the other into the river.

Many died, indeed, by drowning in just this way, weighed
down by their armour as they struck the water, so that they
sank like depth charges. Among these was one of the best-
known citizens of London, one Robert Heysand, a brave
fighter.

[3]

ALL THAT NIGHT the torment endured. If men of either
side, weary, bleeding, endeavoured to crawl back to safety,
leaving the few yards of bridge they occupied to their
opponents, the forward pressure of new troops joining the
battle thrust against them so that they had once more, spent,
panting, to lift up their arms and deal blows that no longer
had the force of an hour before. Dead men were thrust aside
by the brutal feet of men who had tripped over them or caused
their fall. Men died and were prevented from falling because

trapped between furious bodies. The still air was disturbed by groans, shrieks, yells, the spiky palisade of noise reared by the night against it.

Hours passed like minutes for those in the battle. Attack was followed by counter-attack, but as the first streaks of dawn appeared, Gough's men began to tire. They had lost heavily, and many of their leaders had been slain, including Alderman John Sutton and other officers of both the royal and the civic force.

Gradually, while still desperately resisting, the Londoners were forced wholly on to the defensive. The lights of the camp at Southwark became yard by yard more distant to them; the din of war sounded nearer and ever nearer to the men and women in the city abodes lying anxious in their beds. First the Southwark stulpes had to be abandoned, and next a further thrust by Cade swung the conflict towards the wooden drawbridge at the centre, where Gough wished his men to stand. Cade now saw a chance to trap and destroy them. Flinging bundles of flaming material into the houses lining each side of the bridge held by the enemy, he set them on fire, believing that those who did not burn to death would surrender, while others would plunge flaming into the river and die.

The stratagem had dreadful results. Men, their clothing alight, screaming, rushed on to their enemies' weapons rather than endure their agony, and so died miserably to no end. Women in the houses, terrified as the flames leaped from one to the other dwelling, came rushing out, children in their arms, and flying panic-stricken from the struggling, savage men, leaped into the river as their one chance of survival. Others, unable to swim, blinded by the smoke, appalled by the noise, the stench of blood , the clash of steel, the litter of inert bodies, the heat and fire, were too confused and fear-stricken to move, and stayed clutching their burdens while their homes burned behind them. Their smouldering, charred bodies were found next day. Many, no doubt, suffocated in their beds or crouching in the passages of their homes before the fire reached them.

[4]

IF BOTH SIDES paused now and again, there was no genuine cessation of the fighting. The battle now centred on the draw-bridge. Meantime, Cade, who had lost many picked men, decided to rest those who had fought so bravely on the bridge and replace them by fresh troops. These in turn would be supported by men hitherto held in reserve, who, as soon as they arrived on the bridge, would cut and thrust as ably as the more practised soldiery under his command. It was not now a matter of discipline and tactics, but of numbers, will and strength in hand-to-hand contest.

To this end he gave orders that the King's Bench and Marshalsea prisons should be broken open, and any prisoners fit and willing to fight armed and sent into the ranks. A horde of men emerged, some of whom were only too willing to kill or maim those who had put them behind bars, especially as the victory of their liberator would be a guarantee of con-tinued freedom.

Among those who took part in this battle and lived to tell the story was Payn, Sir John Fastolf's man, of whose adventures we have already heard. He had probably been ordered to the bridge to test his declaration, not necessarily untrue, that he was an adherent of Cade's cause. According to his own account he fought for a total period of six hours, and was so severely wounded that he nearly died of his injuries. His sincerity may justly be doubted, because in his celebrated letter he states that Cade's men, during the period when Cade lingered in the south after his victory over the Staffords, burned down his house at Peckham, close to the main road between Maidstone and Tonbridge. This hardly suggests great enthusiasm for the rebel cause. On the other hand, it is just possible that Payn did not know of this domestic catastrophe till much later.

[5]

TRUE TO HIS PROMISE, as soon as dawn gave sufficient light for the purpose, Lord Scales began to bombard the rebels with the guns of the Tower, but there is no evidence that he achieved any great results. The fighting was too close and constricted on the bridge, and any balls that fell on the embattled troops probably killed as many of one side as of the other, for gunfire could hardly discriminate among them at that distance. It is possible, however, although it is not recorded, that this sudden burst of firing had a psychological effect. The knowledge that even after they had won the battle of the bridge, if they did win it, there would still be the hostile Tower, its guns and defenders, to overcome, may have depressed and disheartened the Cade supporters, while at the same time giving fresh heart to the London men.

However, the accession of strength to his force now gave Cade a great chance of victory. Dispirited, weary, over-taxed, and suffering from the loss of so many good officers, with sparks, flame and smoke whirling around them, the groans of the wounded and dying torturing their ears, the wails of the screaming women and the moans of those flying down to death in the river, the stench of burning flesh and scorched timber, all weighing on their spirits, the Londoners, giving ground at last were beaten back right to St Magnus Church corner, where the stulpes on the London side stood. The Kentish men seemed about to prevail. Victory was only a few yards away. One more push and they would be on the north bank, the citizens a fleeing mob, to be hunted down and slain at leisure. Then would London indeed be Cade's, and with her a throne if he coveted it.

But the men of Kent also had come to the end of their

strength. Gough, intelligent, chivalrous, an old and accomplished soldier, with a distinguished record overseas, now played his last card and threw in his own last reserves. Whether he himself led them or not it is impossible to say, but this sudden, renewed onslaught hurled the weary rebels right back until once more they were fighting fiercely to retain a foothold on their own end of the bridge on the Surrey side. Not only was the issue once more in doubt, but also it was now Cade's turn to be threatened with defeat.

His battered, bleeding men were no longer capable of offensive action. He had no reserves left. Nothing could now be done but strive by every means in his power to bring this final attack of his enemies to a halt and save his army from complete destruction.

[6]

HIS ACTION in these circumstances was brilliant, decisive, and illustrates his quick military grasp. By some means he succeeded in setting fire to the drawbridge itself, which burned fiercely with a vast uprush of flame, so that the citizen army pressing towards the Southwark stulpes had to fall back to avoid being incinerated or drowned. Those already fighting at the stulpes were cut off.

Taking fresh heart at the success of their leader's stratagem, Cade's men soon disposed of the trapped units on their side of the bridge, but this was the limit of their success. They could no longer come to grips with their advancing foes. Between the remnants of the two armies lay a wilderness of flame. One pictures them staring across the gap in sullen hate, or with relief that for the time being the fighting was over. Timbers, blazing, cracked and fell, sparks spiralled upwards, and the waters of the river were rosy with reflected light. There were brief red gleams from the metal of armour, steel weapons and the harness of any horses patrolling

the river banks. There was a coiling and swirling of smoke.
Now and again a bearded face was lit up for a second, only
to be obliterated by a fresh billowing of river mist and smoke.
The Thames hissed as it extinguished the burning wood that
fell into it.

Somewhere on the bridge lay now the body of Matthew
Gough, commander of the loyalist army, who had joined
John Sutton in death. With his loss the heart went out of his
troops. They had suffered heavier losses than Cade's men, and
the burning of the drawbridge, whether by design or by an
accidental spark from the ruined houses, must have seemed
the intervention of Heaven to prevent them from achieving
triumph. Nevertheless, some among them watched the flames
with relief, as Cade had done. Now they would not, could not,
be chased down the narrow city streets, hacked and speared
as they ran. No man could leap the chasm between the two
armies. That must have seemed much more important at that
moment than their own inability to invade the Kentish camp.

[7]

THE LIGHT STRENGTHENED as the troops on both sides of the
bridge were still listlessly shooting arrows at one another,
while Scales's guns sent an occasional hot ball splashing into
the river, and while red-eyed, anxious householders peered
out cautiously to make what they could of the crouching,
clustered figures at each end of a severed bridge. The
morning light must have revealed a terrible spectacle.
Everywhere were bodies in all the strange attitudes of death.
Possibly a corpse or two was quietly tipped into the Thames
with a sombre uprush of water as it struck the surface.
Wounded men were dragging themselves as best they could
towards their own friends, sometimes aided, sometimes left
to make their own way. The ashes of the burned houses,
puffed up by the wind, glowed a little or flew into the air to

carry the smell of battle over the whole city. The keen-sighted may have caught a glimpse of handsomely-dressed knights surveying the scene from the Surrey shore, a gleaming, colourful, but somewhat despondent figure standing out prominently among his companions. One or two blackened, singed, bleeding figures may have respectfully made way for this group, or have approached them with reports or requests for orders.

It was much the same on the London side. Malpas and those of his associates left alive may have surveyed the bridge and sent their messengers back to the Tower with prayers for reinforcements or advice.

Both sides were exhausted, and even if it had been possible to resume the fight, there was no longer the desire to do so. The battle had been fought, and neither body could claim that it had won. It was stalemate. Meantime the dead on both sides needed burial, the wounded attention, and the soldiers rest, food and drink. What now? A truce was the obvious answer.

Which side proposed it is not stated. In all probability it was the Londoners, who had started the fight and were therefore the ones who in logic should end it. At 9.0 a.m. on that Monday morning, it was agreed that fighting should cease, on condition that neither army should cross the gap created by the vanished drawbridge nor attack by boat across the river.

The envoys sent by each commander under a white flag had to carry on their discussion by shouting across from one side of the gap to the other, unless, which is unlikely, they took boats and parleyed on the surface of the river. Once the decision to stop fighting was reached, there was no further need to occupy the blackened remnants of the bridge, and the weary Kentish men withdrew, with their comrades on litters or limping beside them, to the Southwark shore, merely posting men on the sound part of their piece of bridge to ensure that the Londoners committed no treacherous act.

Similarly the Londoners retired to their bank of the river, and placed their own sentries in suitable positions.

In every mind must now have been the new question: What comes next? Would Cade make use of the pause to regroup his forces and at a convenient time seek to effect a new entry into the city, his pioneers throwing bridging material across the gap and advancing over it in strength? Would the King and a new army loyal to him come to London and drive the rebels back into the woods?

The position on both sides was now one of great uncertainty. The cutting of the bridge had done more than separate the two armies: it had cut them off to some extent from secret intelligence. Possibly a few spies sailed boats stealthily from one shore to the other, but they ran great risks in so doing, and there was no guarantee either that they would have news worthy of the danger, or live to carry it. Neither party now knew or could divine with assurance the plans of the other.

The Londoners were undoubtedly the more nervous. The battle had hit them hard, because unless loyal armies were genuinely forming in the provinces – of which there was no sure indication – they were in parlous state. The long battle for London Bridge had weakened them more than, or so they believed, it had weakened Cade. They had lost their general and many of their best officers, and there were none of equal stature to replace them.

Cade's men, however, though the Londoners did not know it, had themselves lost much of their enthusiasm for fighting. They, too, had seen many good comrades die, and now that their hated oppressors – Lord Saye, William Crowmer and the rest – had been disposed of, they were less inclined than their leader to kill yet more of their countrymen. If London had still sheltered the other guilty princes they might have been prepared to risk their lives to bring them to justice, summary or otherwise, but these men had fled far beyond their immediate or future grasp; for some of the rebels at least must have guessed what this stalemate at the bridge implied. They saw little point in going on. There may even have been among them some who suspected that Cade had other motives than a noble indignation. As is the way with men on the day of a serious set-back, these began to doubt and fear, and for their own protection, to spread alarm among their fellows. They were rebels, they pointed out, liable, if defeated and captured, to execution for treason. Was it wise to linger on when there was still time to get away?

There may even on that very day have been a tiny trickle of desertions by the faint-hearted, who hoped to escape proscription by going back to their homes and resuming their avocations.

Cade himself cannot but have been dejected as he perceived or suspected the decline in the moral of his forces; but it is to his credit that he himself made no plea for pardon, nor did he disband his men. It must have been a tremendous relief to him when the news came by messenger to the White Hart that his opponents were ready to make peace. For this is precisely what the London party had decided to do. Somehow they must have learned that there was no prospect that the King would come to their aid with a substantial army soon enough to prevent Cade from re-taking the city and beheading all those who had taken the lead in attacking him. They had tried force and failed. The time had come to try subtler means.

The measure of Cade's readiness to accept this offer is indicated by his immediate response. Negotiations would be begun the very next day. The negotiators on the King's side would this time be Cardinal Kempe, Archbishop Stafford and Bishop Waynflete. The place decided upon for the conference was the Church of St Margaret in Southwark. (This church was demolished a considerable time ago. What was then known as St Margaret's hill was once part of the present-day Borough High Street; the existing Church of St George is somewhere near where the old church used to stand.)

In accepting the detested Bishop Waynflete as one of the envoys, it is obvious that Cade was only too eager for peace, and that he had abandoned his dream of becoming England's King. He must have perceived that the one course open to him now was to make the best possible terms for himself and his men. He could no longer dictate, no longer wreak vengeance; but while he still had an army in being and at his back he had a good deal to bargain with.

And so, that drear morning, reeking of death and destruction, the man who for a few days had been lord of London sat down to treat with the very men against whom he had taken up arms. It was the climax of his career, and if it exemplifies anything, it is that the soldier is no match for the politician once he has left the field, and that trust is not a commodity to be placed at the disposal of princes, as shall be seen.

I

TEN

The Great Betrayal

[1]

THE PARLEY between Cade and the dignitaries of the Church represents one of the few occasions when the spiders may be said to have walked into the parlour of the fly; but before it can be discussed, it is necessary to describe the men who came to Southwark and their history.

Cardinal Kempe, himself a man of Kent, was born in 1380 in Wye, in which small town he established a grammar school. Appointed to the Bishopric of Rochester in 1419, he had been by no means a whole-hearted supporter of the detested Duke of Suffolk. On the other hand, he had never allied himself with the Yorkists, to whom he was, and remained throughout his life, inveterately opposed. His mother is said to have been a Lewknor of Sussex, and before his appointment to the see of Rochester, he had held that of Chichester for a short period. Before the conference began, he had become Archbishop of York, and Chancellor in succession to the Archbishop of Canterbury, who had recently relinquished this political post. Kempe had spent the days of the rising under the protection of the Tower, but had not been forced out by the rebels at the time of their removal of Saye. It is said that even when Cade's men were at the gates, he showed no terror. There is a degree of doubt whether he did, in fact, take part in the talks with Cade, but the weight of evidence is on the side of his presence.

John Stafford, Archbishop of Canterbury, the leader of the delegation, was even older than Kempe, who was then nearly seventy years of age. He was a member of one of the junior lines of the Stafford family. Appointed Lord Treasurer in 1422, he became Bishop of Bath and Wells in the following year. The final step in his rise to greatness was his Archbishopric in 1443. He came to this by way of the office of Lord Chancellor, to which he was appointed also in 1443. Both these political offices he had abandoned early in 1450, and he was to die a couple of years after the revolt was over. In contrast to the other two, he had the reputation of being politically neutral, and was not regarded as one of extreme views by either his friends or his enemies. It is unlikely that he played more than a passive part in the negotiations with the Captain of Kent, though his complicity in the cunning stratagem by which the Captain was beguiled is beyond doubt.

William Waynflete, Bishop of Winchester, who has been mentioned earlier, was not only the Provost of Eton College, but had also, like Cardinal Kempe, founded a grammar school in Lincolnshire, where he was born. He was always specially interested in the improvement of educational methods, and later founded Magdalen College, Oxford. A particularly active politician, he became a fervent advocate of the Lancastrian party, so that in later years he was often at loggerheads with the Yorkists. On two occasions, as a result, he had to pay large sums of money to win himself a pardon. It has already been indicated that after the rebellion broke out he went into hiding at the Priory of Holywell, but the Chancellor summoned him thence to the Tower to become one of the trio of emissaries it had been decided to send to the rebel camp.

These men were no amateurs, no innocent children about to beard a vile outcast. They were brilliant, clever men, trained in intrigue and debate, learned, polished, subtle and experienced. They did not go blindly into conference. They had weighed their words, outlined their plans, prepared the instruments with which to outwit their enemy. It is foolish to imagine that Cade confronted weak, unworldly men in his room at the White Hart.

[2]

IT IS AN OLD SAYING that who sups with the devil needs a long spoon. Chamberlain learned its truth when he made a solemn pact with Hitler, at Munich. Roosevelt had unfortunately left the political scene before it was discovered that Stalin had, in the slang phrase, 'pulled a fast one over him'. Though these three fifteenth-century able diplomats and negotiators were at the moment bargaining from weakness, or so they believed, they knew men; they knew the fundamental inexperience in council of the man they had to meet; and in addition, it is not to be supposed that their shrewd eyes failed to appreciate the psychological and military decline in strength of the Southwark camp.

Nevertheless, they did not know, however much they may have suspected it, that Cade, with a shattered, melting and now less trustworthy army, yearning to go home, was as ready for peace as they. When, therefore, these presumably honourable churchmen, ecclesiastical leaders, revered by thousands, made him an offer that seemed both generous and fair, it is hardly to be marvelled at that at the outset he should have leaped at the bait.

Cade was a faithful servant of the Church, and these envoys were invested for him with all the dignity and awe due to leaders of the spiritual body. For this reason it does not appear to have entered his head that this outwardly tempting offer was as cunning a trick as the annals of England can show, and in consequence, he was outwitted.

Before the priests are too severely condemned, however, an effort must be made to see their point of view. Beyond question they had taken a serious personal risk in journeying across the river into Cade's territory. He could have cut off their heads, held them as hostages or to ransom, humiliated and abused them in any one of a hundred ways. That instead he gave them a courteous and honourable reception – as their eventual reports made clear – confirms the point made earlier, that he was a devout Churchman, respecting the hierarchy of the Church, however much they might be and were detested by the lower orders. It is quite on the cards that the churchmen knew this before they ventured to visit him.

To the dignitaries, however, he was a rebel against his anointed King, whose coronation had been performed by the head of their order. Such an offence could not but horrify men of their type at that period. To them Cade was in the literal sense 'a man of the devil', and to be nice in dealing with him was to commit a sin. They had no scruples, therefore, in setting their trap and waiting patiently for him to fall into it. So certain were they of success that they had even brought the trap with them, all ready for use, the fragrant cheese dangling invitation at the end of a hook. And they were not afraid to produce it.

Everything, however, had to be done in good order. Once admitted to Cade's presence, the delegates had first to hear all over again the 'Complaints' of the rebels, which were read out to them with due formality, then presented to them in documentary form for acceptance or rejection. The rebel leader had now to be thrown off guard, led to believe that his cause was now regarded as just, that all he and his men had fought for had been achieved. The 'Complaints' were accepted as formally as they had been put forward, as Richard II in the previous century had accepted the demands of the peasants.

It is not difficult to imagine the delight of Cade, however discreetly hidden behind a mask of impassivity. It seemed as if, after all, he might be back in London before many days. But as the minutes went by, he must have discerned that the matter was not to be all plain sailing. The 'Complaints' had been accepted, true, but it was quickly made evident that a *quid pro quo* was to be demanded.

The envoys insisted that in return for their empty gesture of acceptance, he must immediately disband and disperse his force and send them back to their homes.

This was obviously a 'try-on', to which the Captain was not expected to agree, but which was put forward in the hope of winning from him greater concessions than a more reasonable request would achieve. The weakness of Cade's position is revealed by the fact that he did not reject this stipulation outright; did not get up and leave the conference chamber; but half-accepted it, declaring only that before he gave any such orders, his men must be handed written pardons, signed, sealed and delivered in the proper manner and having the full force of law.

It is permissible to believe that a good deal of feigned discussion and hesitation went on before this concession was granted. Possibly the three churchmen retired to another room to talk over the matter among themselves, concealing that they had come fully prepared and hoping for just such terms. When they came back, they showed their hand. From whatever receptacle had been used to contain them they produced 'Charters of Pardon', one for the rebel chief himself, and a general one for his men. These were to be completed and handed over in exchange for a document agreeing to disband his army, signed by Cade.

[3]

THE SUSPICIOUS READINESS with which these pardons were produced puzzled Cade. It had all been too pat, too smooth, polite and easy. In that moment the first doubts assailed him. Perhaps he caught a sly smile on the lips of the Cardinal, or a glint in the Bishop's eye. He put his thoughts into blunt words. These pardons, though they looked all right, signed as they were by leaders of the faith on behalf of their King, were not quite what he had expected. While he was bound and ready to trust and obey Archbishop, Bishop and Cardinal in all matters spiritual, where such serious things as pardons for rebellion against the Crown were concerned, their signatures had not a proper legal significance. The King could, if he wished, repudiate them. He noticed, moreover, that they had been attested at Westminster, which suggested that the King had neither seen nor approved them, since it was well-known that he was not in that place on the date shown. If, when he returned to London, Henry denied their validity, Cade and his followers, their cohesion lost, would become scattered fugitives, hunted and in peril of their lives.

He put forward, therefore, the perfectly reasonable demand that the pardons should be officially sanctioned by Parliament, and then rendered fully operative by the signature of His Majesty. Only then would he be willing to disband the army in Southwark.

The cunning ecclesiastics were not going to have their bluff called so easily as that. Kempe in particular met Cade's protest by the argument that all this was going to take a terribly long time, since before leaving London the King had dissolved Parliament. In consequence, a new Parliament would have to be convened, which meant a long delay. If these so generous terms were refused, the new army the King was already on the point of bringing to London would have no option but to resume the fight, and the end must be defeat for the insurgents, whose losses, he may have hinted, must be as great as, if not greater than, their own, and whose spirit could not be what it had been. We are bound to assume that some such hocus-pocus as this was employed to force the Captain to accept the pardons as legitimate and sign the paper the priests required.

It was now Cade's turn to go into conference with his

supporters, and it can be taken for granted that they recommended him to agree. He came back to the discussion chamber heavy-hearted, beaten, and with a mandate to accept the offer of pardon for himself and the entire army. This he formally did, and one can visualise the tiny glint of malice and triumph in the eyes of the churchmen as he traced his signature – John Mortimer – on the sheet before him.

[4]

By now, however, Cade had passed from trust to grave and nagging doubt. He perceived that in some way he had been outwitted, though he did not yet comprehend the trick that had been played upon him. He tried once more to insist that his own pardon should be sanctioned by Act of Parliament and royal decree; but now the envoys had the entire rebellion in their tenacious grasp, and were not disposed to let go. He must accept exactly the same form of pardon as his followers. They had no authority to make special exceptions.

At long last, growing steadily more and more aware of the hard and dangerous will behind these smooth and silvery tongues, Cade passed over to them the complete muster rolls so that the pardons could in due course be individually made out. (A general muster meant that all those called up had to be present and fully armed on the day named, but they could not be brought together for any other purpose than a military one.) The meeting then broke up. The Archives of the Corporation of New Romney still have a copy of the original pardon dated 7th July, 1450, and this is made out to John Mortimer.

The three clerics now returned with all solemnity to the Tower, probably in the same sailing boat as that by which they had come, congratulating themselves on having achieved what all the efforts of the soldiers had failed to achieve, the complete disintegration of the rebel army.

News of the official pardons was received with jubilation by many of the men left in the camp at Southwark. Yet the simple country folk, the choleric, honest artisans, farmers and esquires, were not faint-hearts. They believed that the acceptance of their 'complaint' genuinely meant something, backed as it was by the signatures of the three greatest churchmen in England. They could go home now, their duty done, their grievances aired, all injustices on the verge of being eliminated. But the more experienced, abler men became infected with Cade's distrust. During the next twenty-four hours, while the leaders of the revolt considered their personal positions and discussed what they should do, the force began to disperse of its own accord, each man convinced that he could go home and calmly await the better life that was to come. Now England was safe from the vultures who had pecked at her vitals. It was a situation that found its parallel after the Armistice of 1918, when impatient men broke camp, insisted on immediate demobilisation and a year or two later were on the streets looking for jobs.

To those who tried to convince them that they would not get off so easily as they thought, or who sought to keep them in the camp, they replied as men have always replied when sickened of fighting. They had done what they set out to do, and now they weren't going to linger on just to please 'the top brass'. So off they marched to their farms and houses, their ships and shops, happy, singing, glad to be alive with the summer still warming the sweet air, and bloodshed, they believed, behind them for ever . . .

[5]

ALL THAT DAY of the conference and the following day also, Cade lingered at the White Hart, still discussing the future with those closest to him on whom he could rely, and whose danger was as great as his own. Not until the 8th July did he show his hand. By now he had been convinced and convinced the others that once their army had gone, there could be no trust in the pieces of paper in their possession. He may have had spies out, landing secretly on the north bank of the Thames, and listening to the tavern talk or to the more significant words of the wealthier classes. He had decided to form the remnants of the released prisoners, a desperate crowd (who could in any event expect no pardons, since they were not on the original muster rolls, and would almost certainly be put behind bars again, or worse), together with those of his original force who chose to fight with him, into a new army. This, if things went well, might yet win new victories, or, if the worst came to the worst, fly the country.

His first step in this direction was to load all the gold, jewels and other booty he had collected to help pay for the rising, and send these by barge down the river to a supporter he trusted in the Rochester district. There they would be received on his behalf and securely held at his disposal. Meantime, he and his men would march overland in the same direction.

When this decision was announced trouble arose, because those of his lieutenants who had made up their minds to go home believed themselves justified in claiming a proportion of this loot. Quarrels broke out, and it is conceivable that the treasure was secretly packed in just such a chest of the period as may be seen to this day in the church at Ashford, made of pitch pine, bound with semi-circular iron hoops, with a loop in the centre through which a bar is passed to secure it, and carried by means of rings fixed to the ends. Then under cover of darkness the chest was put aboard a barge and sent down river.

While this argument was still going on in Southwark, Cade received on or about 8th July news that completely destroyed whatever hopes he had of making a fresh assault on London. The prelates had tricked him! The pardon he held had been carefully made out in the name of John Mortimer, but now

the Government were claiming, for the first time, that the
Captain of Kent was no true member of the Mortimer family
but a bastard commoner of the name of John or Jack Cade.
Any pardon unwittingly granted to the man who had called
himself John Mortimer could not be regarded as applying
to an impostor named Cade, who merely pretended to be a
Mortimer.

Stowe says that this discovery was made (or announced)
after and not before the pardons had been granted, but if so,
it proves how good Cade's claim to blue blood was. It is,
however, an improbable statement, because it was common
knowledge by the time of the battle for the bridge that whatever blood ran through the Captain's veins, he was not a
legitimate member of the house of Mortimer, and could not
truly claim the family name.

For the moment, however, despite this ominous announce-
ment, there was no suggestion that the pardon had been or
was about to be withdrawn. Nevertheless, Cade was convinced that he had been deliberately tricked into disbanding
his army, and that sooner or later the authorities would strike
at him.

The Government must have hoped that Cade would now
do exactly what he was, in fact, planning to do: fly the
country. This would make it unnecessary for them to take full
advantage of their verbal quibble. They were too sagacious
to have illusions. They knew full well that honest men would
consider their disavowal of Cade's pardon a piece of dis-
honourable trickery. Whatever his faults, however absurd his
pretentions, Cade had put up a good fight and treated his
enemies honourably, if in his view they deserved it. If he left
the country, he would be out of their way, an exile discredited
for the rest of his life, for they could then freely spread their
slanders and distortions.

They had another surprise for him up their sleeves, too.
They had been careful to pardon *by name* only the principal
figures behind Cade, those propertied supporters of the rising

whose lands could be confiscated if they caused further annoyance. The official pardons record no names of the masses *without* property. By this means they prevented the Kentish leader from ever again troubling the peace of the land, since a second sacrifice of their all was hardly to be expected of these landed men.

Meantime, the moment the rebels had abandoned their camp at Southwark and set off on their long march, the order went out that the heads of Saye and Crowmer were to be removed from the bridge, and those taken down by the rebels restored to their original positions. The bodies and heads of the two principal victims of the revolt were now decently buried at Greyfriars. The city breathed out its relief at 'the end of the affair', and the normal daily lives of her inhabitants were resumed. The litter of bodies was tidied up and more graves dug to receive them; the damage to London Bridge was repaired, at first temporarily and then more permanently; the stench of burning and of spilled blood departed; a trickle of folk flowed once more to and fro from the south bank to the city and back again. Messengers rode urgently northwards to notify the King that all danger was at an end. One envisages a slow drift of disillusioned, dispirited, uneasy men from Kent back to their starting-points, accompanied for a time by their Sussex allies, until these departed on their own separate journeys. The men of Essex had already disappeared. Doubtless few of those who travelled homewards had anticipated seeing again or so soon the calm dwellings they had rashly left.

ELEVEN

The Mysterious Attack

[1]

THERE MUST NOW be related the most mysterious and hitherto imperfectly explained incident in the whole of Cade's career. The explanation offered in the following lines is put forward as the only one that can be logically deduced from the available evidence, and is based on personal examination of the terrain concerned and of the facts as we have them. It is original and not to be found in any of the meagre literature covering the period. There can, of course, be no guarantee that it is correct, but whenever it has been propounded to those of the writer's acquaintance who are professional historians it has been considered reasonable and consistent with both the character of the rebel leader and with the known events.

The reader must, however, consider such arguments as are brought forward in favour of the theory that follows, and form his own opinion.

First, the movements of the Captain of Kent must be traced as he broke camp and left the inn at Southwark. He and his band took the main road eastward, passing through Deptford, where a ford crossed the Ravensbourne before it emptied itself into the Thames. It is just possible that they rode past Sayes Court, a mansion belonging to the Duke of Sussex, which was later to house both John Evelyn, the diarist, and

141

Peter the Great of Russia, before being demolished in 1787.
They may even have forced the occupants to provide them
with food and water.

By way of Shooter's Hill and Dartford, with its fine stone
church and Augustinian nunnery, he arrived in Rochester,
probably on the 9th July. Here he appears to have stayed for
at least two days. The chroniclers do not say why, but a
modern writer has put forward the theory that Cade hoped
to make the town, whose Mayor, John Cokerham, a merchant,
was one of his supporters, a centre of resistance from which
he could operate while fashioning a new army.

This, however, though a gallant attempt to solve the
mystery, is not convincing. It is more probable that the halt
was made for the purpose shortly to be described.

It so happens that after his sojourn at Rochester, Cade for
some extraordinary and unknown reason moved northwards
and attacked the castle of Queenborough with all the forces
remaining under his command.

Built a little less than a hundred years before (1361), this
castle played now its one serious part in English history
before being pulled down in Cromwell's time because it was
not worth the money its repair would have cost. It has never
been easy to understand why this petty fortress should have
been attacked. Rochester Castle, past which the rebel force
would have had to go, would have been a much more suitable
centre for recouping his strength, had this been Cade's
intention. It commanded the bridge over the Medway, and
being larger, better built and more defensible than the other,
would have been the obvious choice.

It is, therefore, much more reasonable to suppose that Cade
remained in Rochester for three reasons: (1) to renew
contact with his friend the Mayor and ascertain the prospects
of building up a new revolt with fresh levies. In this connection, it must be obvious that the Keeper of Rochester Castle
cannot have been hostile to Cade, for there is no record that
the rebels encountered active opposition from the garrison

there as they crossed the Medway bridge. It is, indeed, doubtful if they could otherwise have crossed it unscathed.

(2) to negotiate for a vessel or vessels to carry himself and his forces overseas; and (3) *to recover the treasure from the barge in which it had been sent down river from London to a suitable port.*

This treasure was *not*, it is here suggested, in Rochester, but in the possession of *the Keeper of Queenborough Castle*, Sir Roger Chamberlayne, to whom, as one of his most trusted supporters, Cade had sent it for safe keeping. Chamberlayne, a Mortimer man, was expected to deliver it up on demand.

On arrival in Rochester, then, Cade would send trusted messengers to Chamberlayne with instructions to hand over the treasure chest to them. He himself would pause in Rochester until they returned. When they came back empty-handed, it would be with bad news. Chamberlayne, though he may have originally been a Cade supporter, had probably had word down river of what had happened in London, and had decided against taking any further part, active or inactive, in the rising. A fleeing rebel, whose head was in peril, was no man for him to follow. He may already have learned of the trick which had put Cade's life at the King's mercy. To hand over stolen money and jewels on which the rebel depended for further revolt or for escape abroad would be to incur the King's displeasure, even to run the risk of his own pro-scription.

On the other hand, by refusing to restore this wealth to its master, wealth the result of robbery with violence, no doubt, he would at one blow extricate himself from the difficult position in which he had placed himself by tacitly furthering Cade's interests. So he either denied all knowledge of the treasure or flatly refused to surrender it, declaring it the property of the King.

This was a serious and deadly set-back to Cade's plans, leaving him with two alternatives only: either tamely to accept Chamberlayne's defection, dismiss his band in a general *sauve qui peut*, since he was now too poor to charter a ship to carry them all, and himself take to the woods until he could rejoin his friends and find a ship to take him to France; or teach Chamberlayne a lesson, and by a surprise attack on the Castle, regain his misappropriated property and effect escape by sea, his army with him.

[2]

THE CASTLE at Queenborough had been built in the middle of the previous century, when it had a number of 'great' guns, together with nine small ones, delivered from the workshops of the Tower of London. These may have been 'bombards', but this is not certain. In 1374 a good deal of gunpowder was also sent from the Tower to the castle, so that there was obviously a regular connection between them by way of the river. The strength of the place was probably greater, there-fore, than Cade had foreseen, and although it is hinted that only a handful of men made up the garrison (twenty-two), the joint castles of Queenborough and Rochester had been expressly built and gunned to protect the approaches to London from attack by the French coming up river, and would be well-manned.

Queenborough Castle no longer exists and its existence is betrayed only by a hillock and the remains of a moat close to Queenborough railway station. It must have been smaller and far more vulnerable than Rochester Castle, and Cade had no hesitation in deciding on the second of his two alternatives. He would attack.

There is much to support this theory of the cause of his attack. The treasure Cade had sent down river to either Rochester or Queenborough was eventually handed over to or recovered by the Government and disposed of in London, which in itself suggests that it was handed over to their emissaries by some trustworthy person – surely the Keeper of the Castle of Queenborough rather than the suspect Mayor. It is known, furthermore, that at a later date Philip Malpas bought back from the Treasury some of the plunder taken from his house by Cade or his followers.

Again, there is an obscure sentence in Gascoigne which reads 'this captain . . . was mortally wounded by the treason of his servant'. Gascoigne was contemporary with Cade, and his highly-condensed account gives no clue as to the identity of this servant, nor of his act of treason. It could, therefore, mean that the eventual death of Cade was fundamentally brought about by the man he believed his friend, Chamberlayne, whose treachery was his undoing. The person (or persons) who in effect and deed killed Cade was certainly in no way treacherous, since he was merely doing his duty as a Sheriff or officer of the law, and had had no part whatsoever in the rising. Nor is there any record that Cade was accompanied by a friend during his last flight.

Of course, Gascoigne may have implied that the man who actually killed Cade was a former member of his army who had joined the Sheriff's posse and led him to Cade's refuge. This may be true, but it is the only such indication to be found anywhere, and does not appear likely.

There is another point. The chronicles show some confusion between Rochester and Queenborough, its neighbour. For example, John Cokerham is sometimes called the Mayor of Queenborough instead of the Mayor of Rochester. It may well be that it was Cokerham in Queenborough who was refused the treasure by Chamberlayne and therefore urged Cade to attack the Castle and recover it.

It is known that the Duke of York received £114 1s. 0d. as recompense for the theft of 'jewels of gold and silver' belonging to him and stolen by Cade from Malpas's house, where they may have been lodged for safe keeping or, more probably, held as pledges against a loan of ready cash. These 'jewels' were 'delivered into Receipt of Exchequer' and sold

K

for the sum mentioned. Obviously, therefore, the treasure existed and had by then been sent back to London.

[*3*]

To RETURN to the known and leave the conjectural, Cade attacked the Castle on 10th or 11th July, some say with a large force, some with a small. The truth lies probably between these two versions. There is a suggestion that a number of local seamen took part in the affray.

The attack was a complete failure. Cade had no experience of storming a defended fortress – which may in part explain his failure to assail the Tower of London – and at the end of the day he had not only lost many men, but also two at least of his more dependable remaining officers: Geoffrey Kechyn and Captain Boucher, who were taken prisoner. The shattered force withdrew in defeat, and now flight alone remained for the attackers. For all practical purposes the insurrection was over.

This 'gratuitous attack', as one writer terms it – a term this account denies – gave the authorities something they could not have anticipated, but must have welcomed with delight. Now they could do what they had all along been waiting to do. By keeping his force under arms and attacking a royal fortress, the Captain of Kent had committed an act that in itself invalidated the 'pardon' granted to him, whether he were truly a Mortimer or merely the commoner, Cade. So, with an air of sublime innocence that can have deceived none but the simple for whom it was intended, they published a writ and proclamation categorically denying that Mortimer was any other than Cade, as if they had known this from the very beginning.

This writ was published immediately after the attack, and probably on the 12th July, but internal evidence suggests that it had been held in readiness for some days. In substance it repeats the legend that Cade, who is given this name for the first time, had been Dacre's man, had murdered a pregnant servant maid, fled to France, and caused a rebellion on his return. It then goes on to complain that he refused to consider the King's pardon valid without Parliamentary confirmation, which was unnecessary, as the King had the right to pardon crimes and offences of any kind. Its final grievance is that the Captain of Kent, so-called, was trying to foment a new rising.

If this writ had not already been prepared, there would surely have been some reference to the wanton attack on a royal fortress. There was none. The conclusion must be that Cade's proscription had been contemplated from the time of the stalemate at London Bridge, and in all probability he had learned of this from his friends in the city. Hence his desperate last throw, taken with full knowledge of the risks he ran; the flight from Southwark and the onslaught on Queenborough.

The writ declared, furthermore, that no subject of the King must henceforth believe, accompany, help or feed the rebel chief. Anyone was entitled to take him prisoner, and bring him dead or alive to the King or his Council, and such an act would earn a reward of 1,000 marks. The capture of any of his followers would earn 5 marks. No-one was to accept orders from Cade, and all castles, ministers and officers of Kent were to arrest anyone who did.

Cade had remained in Rochester for a day after the defeat of his men, and it is possible that he and his lieutenants now quarrelled violently over the course to be followed. The ferry at Tilbury had been out of action ever since the rising, owing to the disturbances, so there was no chance of an easy escape across the estuary to Essex. Every man's hand was now, in theory, against the erstwhile leader, and he could not be sure that one of his own followers, tempted by the price placed upon his head, might not betray him.

He decided to escape, disguised, perhaps, and alone. He

may have been left in the lurch by those who had accompanied him thus far, or he may magnanimously have considered that it was no longer right for him to place them in further danger by an association with him now that he was a wanted man. Reports had already reached him that his movements were being watched, and that a posse under a determined officer was moving on Rochester. So on the day the King's writ was issued and posted up, he mounted his horse and abandoning the Kentish shore, turned inland and began his last ride. The man who had been lord of London for a handful of days, who had held a kingdom in his grasp, was now a fugitive galloping for his life.

TWELVE

Death in the Afternoon

[1]

ON CADE'S HEELS was one who had made up his mind to bring him to justice. This man was Alexander Iden, described in the documents as 'a Squire of Kent'. He appears to have had some connection with the sea, and may have been instructed to keep a close watch on the Kent country to prevent the rump of the rebel force from re-establishing themselves in some well-fortified position and fomenting new disturbances. It may also have been assumed or known that Cade still had his treasure with him, and he was expected to secure all or some part of this.

Iden's home was, by family tradition, the village of Iden in Sussex, and by this same tradition the family house was at Motes. Assuming that this legend is true, he was a Sussex man rather than from Kent, though the distance separating Motes from Kent was no more than a mile. The Idens were an extremely old and wealthy family, first heard of at Rolvenden in Sussex. Alexander is often given the title of Sheriff of Kent, at this period having been appointed to the position in succession to the previous Sheriff, William Crowmer, beheaded by the rebels. Nevertheless it is hardly likely that his appointment had been made and confirmed during the short space of time between 4th July, when Crowmer met his death, and the 12th, when Cade fled. In fact, a note in the Pipe Roll establishes his accession to the office of Sheriff as occurring in the Michaelmas term of 1450. (He was still Sheriff in 1457). The title was given to him in error too soon by those who wrote of these events at a much later date.

At the time of the rising Iden was living at the Manor of Ripley Court in the parish of Westwell, Kent. It has been suggested that he also owned land in the Sussex district of Heathfield. Crowmer's widow, the daughter of Lord Saye, was as unpopular as her dead father, but Iden married her after the rising was over. It was probably to win her favours that he pursued her father's executioner with such speed and ruthlessness. His success must have made his wooing agreeable.

The old maps make it obvious that the quickest and simplest path of escape for Cade was through the Weald of Kent, where his kinsmen and friends lay, and where he might hope for shelter until such time as he could take ship to France. This, however, was precisely the route he knew his enemies would expect him to take. He did not take it. Instead, he chose a devious path which branched off the main road and led him towards Sussex, where he had once lived, perhaps, and where he had friends who had fought by his side. The Sussex men had come later to the battles than the men of the neighbouring county. Less exhausted and disillusioned, they might be willing, if he could but win sufficient breathing space for persuasion, to take up their arms again and defend him from his pursuers. One sharp rebuff administered might suffice to make the Government chary of further pursuit.

So this lonely man rode by day when it was safe, by night when it was not, along the narrower, less frequented byways. He had flung away his gay Stafford armour and put on the sober, inconspicuous dress of a country esquire, or, one historian suggests, of 'a knight of the post'. As the hours went by in hard riding, hastily snatched meals at village taverns, or with his back against a tree in the thick forest, and sleep wherever and whenever he could get it, he must have felt increasingly secure. As far as he could tell, he had not been

followed. No-one had stopped to question him. None seemed
to have recognised him. When the Sussex downs appeared at
long last on the horizon, they must have brought great joy and
reassurance. He was almost out of Kent, and need not fear.

He had not reckoned, however, with the vengeful, im-
placable, tireless, pursuing Iden. Cade must have been
observed and recognised on his long ride by some who knew
him, but whom he himself did not know. As Iden's troop
clattered on from Rochester, whispers of the lonely horseman
and the route he had taken must have reached him, either
volunteered or obtained by persuasion, gold, threat or more
brutal methods. Iden gave himself and his men no rest, but
indefatigably tracked the fugitive until, about the 13th July,
it is said, he ran Cade to earth.

Shakespeare makes Cade hide for five days in the woods
'and durst not peep out for all the country is laid for him'.
He climbs over a brick wall into Iden's garden in search of
food, is caught, and slain after a fight because in the weakness
of hunger he cannot properly defend himself. This, of course,
is dramatic licence. Cade did not spend anything like five
days on his flight. There may, however, be a grain of truth in
the suggestion that hunger had weakened him.

The precise point of Cade's capture and death is another
of those tormenting mysteries that surround this medieval
figure. There has raged for decades and still rages a con-
troversy on this subject. The rival candidates for the doubtful
honour are Hothfield in Kent and Heathfield in Sussex. It
would be wearisome to detail the pros and cons, turning on
points purely conjectural and based rather on legend and
wishful thinking than on fact. All things considered, the
weight of evidence lies on the side of the theory that a
'garden' in the Heathfield area saw the tragic death of the
Kentish leader. It is said that he was playing bowls in an inn
garden, when an arrow from Iden's bow pierced him, and he
died. This tradition can be ignored. More plausible is the
suggestion that he took refuge in a house in Heathfield known

as 'Newick' in old title deeds, and later as 'Cade's Castle', which once possessed a moat and still retains a few relics of its existence, at Cade's Corner in Sussex, a small hamlet near Heathfield. A gate near-by is still called 'Iden's Gate'. But even this is an untenable theory. What has lent colour to it is that when Francis Newbery of St Paul's Churchyard bought Bailey Park from Lord Dacre in 1791, he re-named it the 'Heathfield Park Estate'. Newbery was so convinced that it was here Cade met his death that he erected a memorial stone on what he judged to be the site. This still stands at the road-side, approximately 450 yards from Cade Street (sometimes wrongly called Cat Street), which in Saxon times was known as Cart Street, and has obviously no genuine connection with Jack Cade. The stone is about 6 ft in height by 4 ft wide, and carries the following inscription:

'Near this spot was slain the notorious rebel Jack Cade by Alexander Iden, Sheriff of Kent, A.D. 1450. His body was carried to London and his head fixed (with nine of his accomplices) on London Bridge. This is the success of all rebels, and this fortune chanceth ever to traitors.' Some lines in old English appear at the foot.

In the warrant for Cade's arrest he is said to have been living in Sussex in 1449, and the Issue Rolls specifically state, when recording the payment of a sum of money to one Davy for taking part in Cade's capture, that this occurred at Heathfield in Sussex. This seems to the writer conclusive.

[2]

CADE'S BODY was treated as he had treated the bodies of others, being stripped of all clothing and flung naked into an open cart. One account says he was not dead when thrown in, but died on the way back to London. There is no indication that this shameful procession aroused either abuse or enthusiasm as it travelled back towards the capital. In all likelihood those who saw it slunk away. The cortège passed through Southwark, where only a short time before the rebel leader had held his 'court'. A halt was made at his old resting-place, the White Hart Inn, and here the hostess was summoned and asked if she could identify the body as truly that of John Cade, the rebel Captain. What her feelings were when she did we shall never know. Unnamed, she passes from history, but it is not necessary to invent for her a sorrow or a scorn she did not necessarily feel.

The dreary journey ended after the party had wound through the stinking alleys and reached the King's Bench prison. Here the body was removed from its cart and allowed to remain from the evening of the Monday till the evening of the following Wednesday. It was not seen again until the executioner had severed the head from the shoulders and quartered the body. This grisly work done, the horrid, mutilated remains were thrown on to a hurdle, the head being so placed that it rested on the breast and the hurdle was then dragged through the narrow streets of Southwark, over the charred, battered, but temporarily repaired, London Bridge, and thence to Newgate jail, by way of the congested, jeering streets of the city.

The old precept of eye for eye and tooth for tooth was greatly respected at the time, and to the victors there was no sin or offence in ensuring that Cade's own head should gruesomely decorate the very bridge on which he had impaled the heads of Saye and Crowmer. This was done, and on the 16th July, those crossing the Bridge could see the proud head, as it had once been, looking towards that fair county from which it had marched – Kent.

Where the savagery of the times is best exemplified is not in this characteristic judicial sentence, but in the way in which the quartered corpse was later treated. Hacked into four pieces, the body was sent four separate ways to four separate towns, as a salutary reminder to all those who had rebelled or might be tempted to rebel again. One piece was despatched to the Constable of the hundred of Blackheath; one to the Mayor of Norwich; one to the Mayor of Salisbury (where, it will be recalled, a Bishop had been murdered at the altar); and one to the Bailiffs of Gloucester.

Presumably Norwich was chosen because it was the principal town of East Anglia, and might therefore be expected to cover the rebels of Suffolk and Essex. For their expenses in despatching these dismal relics, Thomas Canynges and William Hulyn, Sheriffs of London, were awarded sums of money by the Government. In their requests for these payments, the two Sheriffs mention that no other persons either dared to or would carry the head and quarters for fear of their lives.

The King's Council officially thanked Iden for his services on the sea and for taking Cade, and awarded him and other persons of the County of Kent sums of money amounting to just over £433. The King himself gave £20 to John Davy for helping to take Cade. Iden also received £13 6s. 8d. from the King for taking a follower and a principal lieutenant of Cade's known as Robert Spencer. It is said that he (Iden) was also made Keeper of Rochester Castle, with an annuity of £36 as salary, out of which he had to pay £16 for repairs.

It did not take long for the Court to send to Queenborough or Rochester for Cade's goods and cash, released for the purpose, it has been earlier suggested, by Chamberlayne. There is a record of what was found there, in a wooden box in a green chest carrying the sign 'Cade otherwise called Mortimer'. This sign would almost certainly have been affixed by the Keeper of Queenborough Castle, since it is improbable that Cade's known ally in Queenborough or Rochester, the Mayor of that town, would have done this. The treasure was collected by Sir Thomas Tyrell and Richard Waller, an Esquire, and for their 'costs and expenses', these men were allotted £5 13s. 9d. To make sure, however, that nothing was subtracted, the Cardinal Archbishop of York accompanied them, and was given £20 for his trouble on the 19th July.

When examined, the treasure was found to comprise two

large baskets used for holding large quantities of goods; a couple of chests; some gilt and silver salt cellars; a golden chalice studded with pearls; a dozen small silver dishes; two large silver trays of the type known as chargers; three chased cups, knives and spoons; a cruet; a table carrying on it a representation of the Crucifixion; a gallon-sized lidless silver pot; a silver pot holding a quart; an old vestment; a pair of sheets; a small piece of ermine; nine lengths and remnants of silk with golden threads interwoven with it; and a black remnant of a kind of velvet.

Some of these items may have been for use in, or had already been used in, religious services. On 29th August all these goods were put up for sale, and as we have seen, Malpas bought back some of his original property for £114.

Chamberlayne, the defender of Queenborough Castle and preserver of the treasure (though this is not expressly stated) was not forgotten when the various rewards were handed out, and received the sum of 40 marks (about £23) in *part* payment. Is it absurd to suggest that the balance was paid to him when the proceeds of the sale had been determined?

[3]

THE SPECTACLE of a severed head looking out towards Kent, the sight of a quartered body, may not at once have achieved the complete pacification they were expected to ensure. One of those captured at Queenborough was William Parmenter, who was placed in the custody of Thomas Waryn, for which Waryn was awarded £27 10s., shared by himself and twenty-four others, at the rate of one shilling a day for himself and eightpence a day for the others, the period of custody being 32 days. Parmenter was imprisoned first in Windsor and then in Winchester Castle.

He appears to have escaped or been released, and calling himself 'The Captain of Kent', as his master had done before him, gathered together a small force of insurgents and fomented new disturbances at Faversham. There is, however, not much evidence for this minor incident, and it is more likely that the story arose from the mention, in the award to Waryn, of Parmenter as 'the Captain of Kent'. He may have given himself this title while still in custody, either to make it easier for Cade to escape, or, having learned of his leader's death, because he regarded himself as the legitimate or potential successor to the title.

Two other men of Cade's party were beheaded, drawn and quartered – Nicholas Jakes and John Ramsey, a wine-drawer. Jakes's remains were sent to Chichester, Rochester, Portsmouth and Colchester. Ramsey's went to Stamford, Coventry, Newbury and Winchester. It has been said with some justice that the wide dispersion of these remains is ample evidence that the disaffection was widespread, and Cade's rising was merely its outward expression.

Sidelights on the rising are also to be obtained from other small rewards of which record exists. One pound, for example, was paid to John Solers, who had been sent specially on un-specified business to John Cade at Blackheath, presumably to obtain and send back secret reports, for it is explained that he had suffered some 'damage to his goods'. (He may have been detected and roughly handled before being thrown out of the camp.) Fifty pounds was the reward of Thomas Yerde, Sheriff of Surrey and Sussex, for raising a body of men and marching them to Blackheath to fight the rebels as part of the royal force. Lancaster King of Arms received £26 13s. 4d. to recompense him for injuring two horses and hiring others while riding from Leicester to London, Daventry and elsewhere, evidently with the royal proclamation, because the ride is known to have taken place while the revolt was still in progress.

So ended in death and failure, as, in the previous century, the rebellion of Wat Tyler had ended, the insurrection of Jack Cade, who, for a few days, was lord of London and might have been England's king.

THIRTEEN

Aftermath

[1]

ON 1ST AUGUST, 1450, a Royal Commission was despatched into Kent to inquire into various 'offences' that had been committed in that county. It was primarily designed to bring to justice those rebels who had remained under Cade's command during and after his journey through Deptford to Rochester and beyond. It was an impressive body, this Commission, headed by the Duke of Buckingham (who died in battle ten years later), and, as ever, John Kempe, Chancellor and Archbishop of York. With these went the Archbishop of Canterbury; the Bishop of Winchester; Ralph Boteler of Sudely; John Prisote, Chief Justice of Common Pleas, a man notorious for his partiality; Peter Arferne, Chief Baron of Exchequer; Sir Thomas Fulthorpe; Nicholas Assheton and John Portington, Justices of Common Pleas; William Yelverton and Richard Bingham, Justices of the King's Bench; Robert Danvers, who was made a Justice of Common Pleas immediately after, and who had, as is earlier stated, served as a judge at the Guildhall during Cade's occupation of London; William Wangford, later made Sergeant-at-Law; Thomas Burgoyne and William Liaken, afterwards to become Justices of the King's Bench; and finally, John Fortescue, Chief Justice of England. Fortescue was one of the three judges Cade had refused to accept when he first suggested to the

King a judicial inquiry into the grievances of his countrymen.

Here was indeed a wealth of learning and law. The Commission opened its proceedings at Canterbury, and the first thing it did was to condemn and execute eight of Cade's followers. (Incidentally, there is to this day a Gallows Common at Sevenoaks). Whether those executed had 'pardons' or not is not known.

Later, the Commission, which appears to have been peripatetic, moved to Rochester, and from there, into other parts of Kent and Sussex. It was essentially punitive in conception and deed. One seeks in vain for some indication that any attempt was made to inquire into the foundation or otherwise for the grievances that had brought about so serious a rising.

The area from which Cade had drawn his support covered the principal foci of trade and manufacture. These were four in number: (a) the southern outskirts of London and the Thames Estuary, from Blackheath in Surrey through Dartford and Chatham to Gillingham; (b) that area that had suffered most from the raids of the French, losing both possessions and trade, namely Sheppey and Faversham, Sandwich, Rochester and the Isle of Thanet; (c) those who lived on or near the great road which ran from London to the coast, covering Wrotham, Maidstone, Sittingbourne, Ashford, Canterbury; (d) the Cinque ports and the Kent and Sussex coasts. These last two were by far the largest of the four bodies, and represented what may be termed the shipping and industrial areas. There were also the villages of the Kentish Weald between Cranbrook and Tenterden, the inhabitants of which were actuated mainly by patriotic feeling.

Certain districts, such as Lydd and Hythe, had been cautious, and while not sending their levies to march with Cade, had presented him with complimentary gifts, among which may be mentioned *porpoises*. Lydd, bolder than Hythe, also added a Constable on horseback to 'aspy tythinges of the Captain' – presumably to report on his success or failure.

The charge brought against both Cade and the remnant

that fought at Queenborough was that they made war after
having been pardoned. Many pardons had, in fact, been
issued, and were later *confirmed*, which suggests that all of
them underwent revision and some may have been cancelled.
A list of these was disinterred in the form of a Patent Roll
from the records by W. D. Cooper in 1866 and 1868. It gives
an excellent indication not only of the areas and personages of
the rising, but also of the type of people who took part in it.
The Prior and Convent of Bilsington had to be specially
pardoned for their complicity in the murder of Moleyns,
Bishop of Salisbury, and Ayscough. Thomas Bigg of Lambeth,
a yeoman, was outlawed. In the church at Fletching there is a
brass to a local glover who was a member of Cade's army.

But what of John Payn – whose survival of the Battle of
London Bridge has been noted? Payn was impeached and
arrested by the King's Commons and held in Marshalsea at
the request of John Lowe, Bishop of Rochester (which
suggests that Payn had actually accompanied the rebel force,
willingly or otherwise, to that town). He was accused of
riotous conduct after 7th July and until 10th July, 1450.

For a time it looked as if he, too, would be executed, then
drawn and quartered, but one divines that once more his
plausibility came to his aid, so that the amiable rogue was
granted a pardon. Sir John Fastolf, his master, is believed to
have served as the prototype for Shakespeare's Falstaff. He
was reputed to be both coward and braggart, and Cade held
him partly responsible for the loss of Normandy. He died in
1459, aged ninety, at his residence at Ebington, where he
is buried in the churchyard. After the rising he was exiled,
later pardoned, and his estates were restored to him.

The Duke of Somerset seems to have joined the Commission
in Kent at a late stage, together with Fastolf himself, because
he was awarded £200 for helping to establish peace and
tranquillity, and for chastising and punishing the offenders.
This was an advance paid to him by a goldsmith on account of
twenty marks a day, his fee for attending the sittings.

Six horses belonging to Cade (perhaps those extorted by him from the Lombards) were lent out to the Keeper of the Privy Seal to help him on a journey he was making at the King's request.

[2]

THE AUTHORITIES having now arbitrarily executed those they most feared, felt a need to ensure that their actions had the full sanction of Parliament. To this end on 9th November they brought in a Bill of Attainder against Cade, which was speedily passed. The terms of the eventual Act were that Cade was a 'false traitor' who had sought the death of the King and the destruction and subversion of his realm. Levying a great number of the King's subjects, he had raised an insurrection and made war. Although he was dead and his body had been exhibited, he had not been 'officially' punished by the supreme law of the land.

In consequence, it had been decided that to put traitors in fear in time to come, he be convicted of treason, and therefore all goods, lands and tenements, rents and possessions owned by him on 8th July and thereafter, should be forfeited to the King. In addition his blood was to be considered 'corrupt and disabled', and he was to be called a false traitor for ever.

Had Cade been the illiterate, penniless lout suggested by Shakespeare and others, it is hardly likely that the Crown would have taken the trouble to declare forfeit his 'goods, lands and tenements, rents and possessions'. Obviously he was a man of substance. Similarly, the mention of his 'blood' in itself suggests that the Government knew full well he was one whose lineage might have some future claim to consideration unless by law this could be rendered impossible.

Cade was, indeed, a name of some antiquity, common in Surrey, Sussex and Kent, where it is found in the twelfth century as well as the thirteenth. An Edward Cade was an

Alderman of the Hundred of Faversham in the reign of Henry III. Two Cades are said to have been parishioners of Marefield, in the 16th century. There was also a Cade who owned a boat plying up and down the Thames at the very time of Cade's rising. Is it too fanciful to suggest that he may have taken the booty down river to Queenborough, or been a possible arranger of passage for Cade's army to the Low Countries?

The Act was, of course, passed, and the Court could then proceed with greater freedom. In the January of 1451, the King himself went to Canterbury and Sussex to preside over the sittings of the Royal Commission, still delving into the facts of the insurrection. The Justices during that time condemned twenty-six more men to death, and His Majesty had no hesitation or remorse in giving his royal assent to this judgement. The day was thereafter known for a long period as 'The Harvest of Heads'.

On returning from Canterbury, Henry was met at Blackheath by a small body of men, clad in their shirts only, who knelt down in the mire of the road, bowed repentant heads, and begged for mercy. They were pardoned. The King had, however, planned to ride in state through the City of London after this assertion of both his power and his clemency. To cow dissidents, therefore, some of the heads that had fallen – the reports say at Rochester – were transported to London Bridge, where they joined the head of their leader. One record gives the total number of heads decorating the bridge on that day as thirteen.

Sir William Oldhall, Speaker of the House of Commons in the Parliament of November, 1450, was outlawed in 1453 as a follower of Cade. Another who escaped death was William Cayens, who claimed sanctuary in St Martin's Church when the rebels were scattered, and although the Court wished to have him dragged out and executed, the Dean repaired immediately to the Palace with the charter he possessed which gave him the right to shelter offenders against the law. He

L

succeeded in establishing his authority in this respect, and Cayens was allowed to remain on condition that he committed no future treason. In later years he received a full pardon, and even achieved some favour with the King.

Another interesting lawsuit arose directly out of the rising. Richard Horne and John Judde brought an action against Lawrence Stokewode of London, an Alderman appointed to that office by Cade. The complaint was that a certain Simon Shipton, 'Sworn man of the traitor, Jack Cade', terrified Judde's wife by menaces in her own home, and compelled her to give him money. This, it was alleged, was because Horne and Judde had been sent by the King in two barges to keep open the river for the transport of victuals, and to stop Londoners from going by river to join the Captain.

It was also alleged that Stokewode and his associates tried to persuade Horne to kill Judde for twenty shillings and some extras. Other brutal deeds are mentioned.

This legal action, if justified, had probably nothing whatsoever to do with Cade himself, but is valuable as showing that advantage was taken of the rising by unscrupulous men to extort money by threats. Judde later became Master of the King's Ordnance, but in 1459 met his death at the hands of the Yorkists when taking munitions to the King. Stokewode was a drysalter of some standing, and was probably one of Cade's city allies.

[3]

THE PARDONS issued by the Government included a number of East Greenwich and Dartford women, who may have sold food and other supplies to Cade's forces as they passed through or may have sheltered and hidden them on their return. Also pardoned were the Bailiff of Folkestone and the Mayor of Queenborough. Four Canterbury and Rochester men were ultimately to become Members of Parliament some time after they had been pardoned. Another interesting personage who lived to achieve high office after being pardoned was Sir John Cheney, an M.P. for the City of London in 1449, uncle by marriage of Margaret Beaufort. He had fought at Agincourt. For him to have taken up arms against the son of Harry of England must have been a terrible decision to make, and points clearly to the depth of feeling among the gentry regarding the condition of England at the time. Cheney was pardoned, probably because of his age and his previous good record. He became a Sheriff twice, once in 1455 and again in 1464. His son fought in the Battle of Bosworth Field and was popular with Henry VII.

Despite all their severe measures, their parade of the King's person, and the occasional mercy they showed to chosen individuals, the Government were still uneasy. They must have known that the suppression of the revolt had by no means eliminated the animosity against them felt by the common people and the local Squires. In 1452 when Parliament was in session at Reading they passed, therefore, a further Act of Attainder. This far outdid the first in heaping opprobrious words upon the long-since vanquished Cade. In substance it repeats what the first Act said, only more so. Its real and stated purpose was, in essence, to annul any acts done or appointments made by the Captain during his brief period of power. Those interested in the 'official' language of the period may study these two Acts at their leisure in Appendices VI and VII.

With the passing and signature by the King of this Act, the rising may be said to have reached its end. It had lasted from Trinity Sunday until St Thomas's eve, which is the eve of the Translation of St Thomas of Canterbury. The brief expedition to Queenborough was merely a sideshow, of no great significance.

Four years after the second Act of Attainder was signed, the Wars of the Roses officially began, and Englishmen were once more at each other's throats.

Appendix One

Songs and poems levelled against the Government

'*The Corruption of the Times*'
Fulfilled is the prophecy for aye
That Merlin said, and many one mo.
Wisdom is well nigh away.
No man may know his friend from his foe.

Now beguilers do good men rule
Right goes uncounselled all behind.
Truth is turned to treachery's seat,
For now the blind doth lead the blind.

Now the flatterers full gaily go;
Poor men be perished off this land.
Certes, some time it was not so.
But sure all this is sin's message.

Now maintainers be made justices,
And lewd men rule the law of kind.
Noble men be holden wise,
For now the blind doth lead the blind.

The following 'dirge' was sung by the Commons of Kent at the time of their rising under Jack Cade. There are other versions, but the one below is the most complete.

In the moneth of May whan gres growes grene,
    Fragrans in there floures with a swet savour,
Jake Napis in the see a maryner for to bene,
    With his clogge and his cheyne to seel more tresowr.
Such a thynge prykkd hym, he axid a confessour.
    Nycolas of the Towre seyd I am redy here to se;
He was holde so hard, he passyd the same houre.
    For Jake Napes sowle placebo and dirige.

Who shall execute ye feast of solempnite?
Byshoppis and lords as gret reson is,
Monkes, chanons, and prestis, with all ye clergy,
Prayeth for hym that he may com to blys,
And that nevar such anothar come after this.
His interfectures blessid mot they be,
And graunt them to reygne with aungellis,
For Jake Napys sowle placebo and dirige.

Placebo, begynneth the Bishopp of Hereforthe.
    Dilexi, quod ye Bisshop of Chester, for my avaunse.
Hew michi, seyd Salysbery, this game gothe ferforthe.
    Ad Dominum cum tribularer, seyth ye Abbot of Glocester.
Dominus custodit, thus seyth ye Bisshoppe of Rowchestre.
    Levavi oculos meos, seyth Frere Stanbery.
Si iniquitates, seyth ye Bisshop of Worcestre.
    For Jack Napys sowle de profundis clamavi.
Opera manium tuarum, seyth ye Cardinall wysely.

Hath wrong confitebor for all Jake Napis wisdom.
    Audivi vocem, seyd Jhesus on high.
Magnificat anima mea Dominium.
    Now to this dyrgge most we nedys come.
This joyful time to sey brevely,
    ix psalmes ix lessons to sey all and sum.
For Jake Napis sowle placebo and dirige.

Executor of this office dirge for to sunge,
  Shall begynne ye Bisshope of Seynt As.
Verba mea auribus, seythe the Abbot of Redynge,
  For all our hope and joy is come to allas.
Convertere Domine, for us wantyth grace,
  Thow Abbot of Seynt Albanys full sorely synge ye.
The Abbot of the Towre Hyll, with his fate face.
  Tremelyth and quakythe, for Domine ne in furore.

Master Watyr Kyard schall sey ne quando.
  The Abbes of Seynt Alborghe Domine Deus meus in te
    speravi.
Requiem eternam, God grawnt hem to,
  To sey a patar nostar, the Bysshop of Seynt Davi
For the sowles of these wyse and wurthy,
  Adam Molens, Suffolke, Sir Robert Ris, the thre.
And specyally for Jake Napis sowlle that ever was sly,
  For his sowle placebo and dirige.

Rys up, Lord Say, and rede Parce migh, Domine,
  Nichil enim sunt dies mei, that shall thow singe,
The Byssop of Carlyll seyth credo videre
  All fals traytors come to evyll endynge, Dwelle thow shalt
    withe grete mornynge,
Rede Tedet animam meam vite mee,
  Manus tue, Danyell thow shalt synge.
For Jake Napis sowle placebo and dirige.

Qui Lazarum resussistasi, Trevilyan shall synge:
  Hungerford, manus tue fecerunt me,
Uby me absondam, for dred this day.
  John Say singe Dominus regit me;
Nichyll michi deerit for owt that I can se.
  Ad te Domine kevavi, Master Somerset shall rede.
John Oenycoke, Delycta juventutis mee,
  Allas, whither may I fle for dred?

Dominus illuminacio help, for now is ned.
  Seyth Maystar Will Say, I trow it wyll not be.
Credo videre, Sir Thomas Stanle take hede.
  For Jake Napis sowle placebo and dirige.
In memoria eterna, seyth Mayster Thomas Kent.
  Now schall owre treson be cornicled for evar.
Patar nostar, seyd Mayster Gerveyse, we be all shent,
  For so fals a company in Englong was nevar.

The Abbot of Barmundsey, full of lechery,
  Quantas habeo iniquitatys take for thy lesson.
Gabull of the Chancery begynyth Hew michi,
  This is his preve bande and detent of treson.
Home natus de muliere, seyth ye Master of Sent Laurence,
  Repletur multis miseriis, and that shall he wayll,

Of Jake Napes sort that hath don gret offence,
And ever whill he lyved cheff of his counceyll.
  Ne recorderys, Stephem Shegge shall synge.
Quis michi tribuat for wichecraft, seyth Stace,
Domine, non secundum actum meum, for then shall U hynge
For Jake Napys sowle placebo and dirige.

Expectas expectavi, seyth Sir Thomas Hoo.
  Complaceat tibi, begynneth John Hampton.
Beatus qui intelligit and dredit also,
Seyth John Fortescw, all this false treson.
  Sana Domine owre wittes with reson,
The Lord Sudely devoutly prayth.
  Quem admodum desiderat, ye Lord Stowrton,
Sitivit anima mea for hym lyeth.
  The Lord Ryvers all onely seythe
Requiem eternam, God grawnt us to se.
  A patar nostar ther must be in feyth,
For Jake Napis sowle placebo and dirige.

Spiritus meus attenuabytur, Blakney shall begyn.
Pecantem me cotidie, seyth Myners.

Pelle me consumptus carnibus to the nynne,
Robart Horne, alderman, that shall be thy vers.

Requiem eternam for the respons.
Phylip Malpas be thow redy to synge,

It wexyth derk, thou nedyst a scons,
Com forth, Jude, for thow shalt ibrynge.

Quare de vulva eduisti ?
Ser Thomas Tadnam, that rede ye.

Abbot of Westmynstar, com stond by
In thy myter and cope, and sey libera me.

Arys up, Thorp and Cantelowe, and stond ye togeder,
And synge Dies illa, dies ire.

Pulford and Hanley, that drownyd ye Duke of Glocester,
As two traytors shall synge ordentes anime.

And all trew comyns ther to be bolde
To sey Requiescant in pace.

For all the fals traitors that Engelong hath sold.
And for Jake Napis sowlle placebo and dirige.

Finis.

Amen. Writn owt of David Norcyn his booke by John Stowe.

Notes. 'Nycolas of the Towre' was the ship that intercepted the Duke of Suffolk. The Bishop of Hereford was Richard Beauchamp, who became Bishop of Salisbury the same year. The Bishop of Chester, i.e., of Coventry and Lichfield, at that period was William Booth. The Bishop of Salisbury was William Ayscough, who, as stated in the narrative, was murdered soon after Suffolk.

The Abbot of Gloucester was Reginald Butler or Boulers, who became Bishop of Hereford on the 23rd December, 1450. The Bishop of Rochester was John Lowe. Friar Stanbery was John Stanbery, a Carmelite, Provost of Eton, who was nominated by the King to the Bishopric of Norwich in 1445, but was set aside by the Pope. The Bishop of Worcester was John Carpenter. The Cardinal referred to was, of course, John Kempe, Archbishop of York. The Bishop of St Asaph (As) was named Thomas, but his surname has not come down to us.

The Bishop of Norwich at the time of the dirge was called Watyr Kyard, and it is assumed that he is referred to in the song, but it may have been a namesake. There was at the same period a Walter Hert who was Prebendary of St Paul's. The Abbot of St Alborghe was the Abbot of Westminster. The Bishop of St David's was John Delebere. Adam Molens was, of course, the Bishop of Chichester murdered in January 1450. Sir Robert Ris or Rhys was associated with this priest in surrendering Maine to the French.

The Bishop of Carlisle was Nicholas Close. 'Dwelle' is Lord Dudley. 'Danyell' is Thomas Daniel, one of the most hated of the King's counsellors. 'Trevilyan' was John Trevilian, who figures in another political poem of the time as 'The Cornish Chough'. 'Stephen Shegge' may allude to Stephen Slegge, mentioned in the narrative.

Appendix Two

A Proclamation made by Jack Cade, Captain of the Rebels of Kent

THESE BE THE POINTS, causes and mischief of gathering and assembling of us, the King's liege men of Kent, the iii day of June, the year of our Lord 1450, the reign of our sovereign Lord the King xxixth, the which we trust to Almighty God to remedy, with the help and the grace of God and of our sovereign lord the King, and the poor commons of England, and else we shall die therefor.

We, considering that the king our sovereign lord, by the insatiable covetous malicious pomps and false and of nought brought up certain persons, and daily and nightly is about his highness, and daily inform him that good is evil and evil is good, as Scripture witnesses: Ve vobis qui dicitis bonum malum et malum bonum.

Item, they say that our sovereign lord is above his laws to his pleasure and he may make it and break it as him list, without any distinction. The contrary is true, and else he should not have sworn to keep it, the which we conceived for the highest point of treason that any subject may do to make his prince renn in perjury.

Item, they say that the commons of England, would first destroy the king's friends and afterward himself, and then bring the D. of Yk. to be kyng, so that by their fals menace and lies they make him to hate and to destroy his friends, and cherisheth his false traitors. They call themselves his friends, and if there were no more reason in the world to know, he may know they be not his friends by their covetousness.

Item, they say that the king should live upon his commons, and that their bodies and goods be the king's; the contrary is true, for then needed him never parliament to sit to ask good of his commons.

Item, they say that it were great reproof to the king to take again that he hath given, so that they will not suffer him to have his own good, nor land, nor forfeiture, nor any other food but they ask it from him, or else they take bribes of others to get it for them.

Item, it is to be remedied that the false traitors will suffer no man to come to the king's presence for no cause without bribes where none ought to be had nor no bribery about the king's person, but that any might have his coming to him to ask him grace or judgment in such case as the king may give.

Item, it is a heavy thing that the good D. of Glost. was impeched of treason by a false traitor alone, and so sone was murdered and might never come to his answer; but the false traitor Pole was impeched by all the whole common of England, the which number passed a quest of xxiiiM., and might not be suffered to die as the law would, but rather the said traitors of the affinity of Pole that was as false as Fortager would that the king own sovereign lord should hold a battle within his own realm to destroy his people and afterwd. himself.

Item, they say that when the king shall be traitor and whom he will shall be none, and that appeareth hitherto, for if any of the traitors about him would malign against any person, high or low, they would find false means that he should die a traitor for to have his lands and his goods, but they will suffer the king neither to pay his debts with all, nor pay for his victuals nor be the richer of one penny.

Item, the law serveth of nought else in these days but for to do wrong, for nothing is sped almost but false matters by colour of the law for mede, dred and favour, and so no remedy is had in the court of consceince in any wise.

Item, we say our sovereign lord may understand that his false counsel hath lost his law, his merchandise is lost, his common people is destroyed, the sea is lost, France is lost, the king himself is so set that he may not pay for his meat nor drink, and he oweth more than any king of England ought ever, for daily his traitors about him where anything should come to him by his laws, anon they ask it from him.

Item, they ask gentlemen's goods and lands in Kent and call them risers and traitors and the king's enemies, but they shall be found the king's true liegemen and best friends with the help of Jesus, to whom we cry day and night with many M. more that God of his grace and righteousness shall take vengeance and destroy the false governours of his realm that hath brought us to nought and into much sorrow and misery.

Item, we will that all men know that we blame not all the lords, nor all them that is about the king's person, nor all gentlemen nor yeomen, nor all men of law, nor all bishops, nor all priests, but all such as may be found guilty by just and true enquiry and by the law.

Item, we will that it be known we will not rob nor reve nor steal but that these defaults be amended, and then we will go hom; wherefore we exhort all the king's true liegemen to help us, to support us, for whatsoever he be that will not that these defaults be amended, he is falser than a Jew or Saracen, and we shall with as good will live and die upon them as upon a Jew or Saracen, for who is against us in this vade will we mark, for he is not the true king's liegeman.

Item, his true commons desire that he will avoid from him all the false progeny and affinity of the D. of S., the which are openly known, and that they be punished after the law of the land, and to take about his noble person his true blood of his royal realm, that is to say the high and mighty prince the D. of Y., exiled from our soverieng lord's person by the noising of the false traitor the D of S and his affinity. Also to take about his person the mighty prince the Duke of Exeter, the D. of Buck., the D. of Nflk, and his true earls and barons of his land, and he shall be the richest king christian.

Item, the true commons desireth the punishment upon the false traitors, the which counterfeited and imagined the death of the high and mightful and excellent prince the D. of Gl., the which is much to reherse, the wh. D. was proclaimed at Bury openly in the Parlmt a traitor, upon the which qurell we purpose us to live and die that it is false, also our father the cardenall, the good D. of Ex., the noble prince the D. of Warw., the which were delivered by the same means untrue, also the realm of France lost, the Duchy of Normandy, Gascon and Gyan, and Anoy domain lost by the same traitors, and our true lords, knights and squires, and many good yeomen lost and were sold or they went, the which is great pity and great loss to our sovereign lord and to all the realm.

Item, they desyre that all the extortioner might be laid down, that is to say the green wexe, the which is falsely used to the perpetual hurt and distruction of the true commons of Kent; also the extorsioners of the King's Bench, the which is right chargeable to all the commons withouten provision of our sovereign lord and his true council.

Item, taking of wheat and other grains, beef, mutton and other victual, the which is importabel hurt to the commons, without provision of our sovereign lord and his true council, for his cmmons may no longer bear it.

Item, the statute upon the labourers and the great extortioners of Kent, that is to say, Slegge, Crowmer, Isle and Robert Est.

Item, where we meve and desire that some true justice with certain true lords and knights may be sent into Kent for to enquire of all such traitors and bribers, and that the justice may do upon them true judgment, what some ever they be; and that our sovereign lord direct his letters patents to all the people that universal openly to be read and cried, that it is our sovereign lord's will and prayer of all his people truly to enquire of every man's governance and of defaults that reigneth, nother for love, favour, dread nor hate, and that due judgment shall be forthwith and thereupon. The king to keep in his own hands their lands and goods, and not give them away to no man, but keep them for his richnesse, or else our sovereign lord to make his emarme into France, or else to pay his debts; by this our writing ye may conceive and see whether we be the friends ethar enemies.

Item, to sit upon this enquiry we refuse no judge except 111 chief judges, which are false to believe.

Item, that they be gylte wyll wrye against this, but God will bring them down, and that they shall be ashamed to speak against reason, but they will go to the king and say that if they be taken from him that we will put him down, for the traitors will live longer, and if we were disposed against our sovereign lord, as God it forbid what might then the traitors help him?

Item, these defauts thus duly remedied, and from enceforth no man upon pain of death being about the king's person shall take no manner of bribe for any bill of petitions or cause speeding or letting, our sovereign lord shall reign and rule with great worship and have love of God and of his people, for he shall have so great love of his people that he shall with God's help conquer where he will; and as for us, we shall be all ways ready to defend our country from all nations with our own goods, and to go with our sovereign lord where he will command us, as his true liegemen.

Finis.

Appendix Three

*The Bill of Complaints and Requests of the Commons
of Kent*

(1) It is openly noised that Kent should be destroyed with a
royal power, and made a wild forest, for the death of
the Duke of Suffolk; of which the Commons of Kent
were never guilty.

(2) The King is stirred to live only on his Commons, and
other men to have the revenue of the Crown; the which
has caused poverty in his Excellency, and great payments of the people, now late to the King granted in his
Parliament.

(3) That the Lords of his royal blood have been put from
his presence, and other persons of lower nature exalted
and made chief of his Privy Council; the which stoppeth
matters of wrong done in the realm from his excellent
audience, and so may not be redressed as law will, but
if bribes and gifts be messengers to the hands of the
said Council.

(4) The people of his realm be not paid of debts owing for
stuff and purveyance taken to the use of the King's
household, an undoing of the said people, and the poor
Commons of this realm.

(5) The King's menial servants of household, and other
persons, asked daily goods and lands, of impeached or

indited of treason; the which the King granted anon, ere they so endangered to be convicted. The which caused the receivers thereof to enforce labour and means, applied to the death of such people so impeached or indited, by subtile means, for covetize of the said grants; and the people so impeached or indited, though it may be untrue, may not be committed to the law for their deliverance, but held still in prison to their uttermost undoing and destruction, for covetize of goods.

(6) Though divers of the poor people and Commons of the realm have never yet so great right, truth and perfect title to their land, yet by untrue claim of assessment made unto divers states, gentiles and the King's menial servants in maintenance against the right, the true owners dare not hold claim nor pursue their right.

(7) It is noised by common voices that the King's lands in France have been aliened, and put away from the Crown and his lords and people there destroyed with untrue means of treason; of which it is desired enquiries through all the realm to be made how and by whom; and if such traitors may be found guilty, them to have execution of law, without any pardon, in example of others.

(8) Collects of the 15th penny in Kent be greatly vexed and hurt in paying great sums of money in the exchequer to sue out a writ called quorum nomina for allowances of the Barons of the ports, which now is desired that hereafter in the lieu of the collectors the Barons aforesaid may sue it out for their ease at their own costs.

(9) The sheriffs and under-sheriffs set to farm their offices and bailiwicks, taking great surety therefor; the which causeth extortions done by them, and by their bailiffs to the people.

(10) Simple and poor that use not hunting be greatly oppressed by indictments, fained and done by the said

M

sheriffs, under-sheriffs bailiffs and others of their assent, to cause their increase for paying of the said farm.

(11) They return in names of inquests in writing into divers of the King's courts not summoned or warned; where through the people daily lose great sums of money, well nigh to the uttermost of their undoing, and make levy of amersments called the green wax, more in sums of money than can be found due of record in the King's books.

(12) The ministers of the Court of Dover in Kent vex and arrest divers people through all the shire out of Castle-ward, passing their bounds and liberty used of old time, by divers subtle and untrue means and actions falsely fained, taking great fee at their lust, in great hurt of the people in all the shire of Kent.

(13) The people of the said shire of Kent may not have their free election in the choosing knights of the shire, but letters have been sent from divers estates to the great rulers of all the country, the which enforcement their tenants and other people by force to choose other persons than the common will is.

(14) Whereas knights of the shire should choose the King's collectors indifferently, without any bribe taking, they have sent now late to divers persons, notifying them to be collectors; whereupon gifts and bribes be taken, and so the collector's office is bought and sold extortionately at the knights' lust.

(15) The people be sore vexed in costs and labour, called to the sessions of peace in the said shire, appearing from the farthest and uttermost parts of the west unto the east; the which causeth to some men five days journey; whereupon they desire the said appearance to be divided into two parts, the which one part to appear in one place, another in another place, in relieving of the grievance and intolerable labour and vexations of the said people.

The Requests by the Captain of the Great Assembly in Kent

(1) Desireth the Captain of the Commons, the welfare of our sovereign Lord, the King, and all his true Lords, spiritual and temporal; desiring the said Sovereign Lord, and of all his true Lords of the Council, to take in all his domains, that he may reign like a king royal, according as he is born our true Christian King anointed; and who so will say the contrary, we will all live and die in the quarrel as his true liege men.

(2) Desireth the said Captain that he will avoid all the false progeny and affinity of the Duke of Suffolk, the which hath been openly known; and they to be punished after the custom and law of the land, and to take about his noble person the true Lords of his royal blood of this his realm; that is to say, the high and mighty Prince, the Duke of York, late exiled from our own said sovereign Lord's presence (by the motion and stirring of the traitorous and false disposed the Duke of Suffolk and his affinity) and the mighty Princes and Dukes of Exeter, Buckingham and Norfolk, and all the Earls and Barons of this land; and than shall he be the richest Christian king.

(3) Desireth the Captain and Commons punishment upon the false traitors, the which contrived and imagined the death of the high and mightful prince, the Duke of Gloucester; the which is too much to rehearse, the which Duke was proclaimed as a traitor. Upon the which quarrel, we purpose all to live and die upon that it is false.

(4) The Duke of Essex, our holy father the Cardinal, the noble Prince, Duke of Warwick, and also the realm of France, the Duchy of Normandy, Gascogny and Guien, Anjou and Maine, were delivered and lost by the means of the said traitors: and our true Lords Knights and Esquires, and many a good yeoman lost and sold ere

they went, the which is a great pity to hear of the great and grievous loss to our sovereign Lord and his Realm.

(5) Desireth the said Captain and Commons, that all the extortions used daily among the common people might be laid down; that is to say the green wax, the which is falsely used to the perpetual destruction of the King's true Commons of Kent. Also the King's Bench, the which is too grief-ful to the shire of Kent without provision of our sovereign Lord and his true Council. And also in taking of wheat and other grains, beef, mutton, and all other victual, the which is importable to the said Commons without the brief provision of our said Sovereign Lord and his true Council – they may no longer bear it. And also unto the Statute of Labourers, and the great extortioners, that is to say the false traitors Sleg, Cromer, Isle and Robert Est.

Appendix Four

Writ and Proclamation by the King for the taking of Cade

FOR SO MUCH as one John Cade, born in Ireland, which calleth himself John Mortymer, and in some writing calleth himself Captain of Kent, the which John Cade the last year before his dwelling in Sussex with a knight, called Sir Thomas Dacre, slew there a woman with child, and for that cause too the greeth of the church and after, for that cause forsware the King's land; the which John Cade also after this, was sown to the French port, and dwelled with them, which hath now of late time (to the intent to enrich himself by robbing and despoiling of the King's liegemen, and it is now openly known to bring himself to great and high estate) falselie and untruly deceived many of the King's people, and under colour of holy and good intents, made them assemble with him against the King's regality and his laws, naught setting by the King's grace and pardons, granted not only to him but to all the King's subjects, the which by his deceit have assembled with him, the which he with great reverence received on Monday last passed, and so did all that were assembled with him. Notwithstanding all this, he laboreth now of new to assemble the King's people again, and to that intent beareth them on hand, that the King's letters of pardon granted to him and them, be not available nor of none effect, without

181

authority of Parliament; whereas the contrary is true, as it is openly known by that, that the King granted from time to time, his charters of pardon to such as him list, of manner of crimes and offences both general and special.

The King therefore willeth and commandeth that none of his subjects give faith nor credence to the said false information of the said false traitor, nor accompany him in any wise, nor comfort, nor sustain him nor with his victuals, nor with any other thing; but will whosoever of the King's subjects may take him, shall take him; and that whosoever taketh him, and bringeth him, quick or dead, to the King or his Council, shall have 1,000 marks for his labour truly paid him, without fail or delay, by the promotion of the King's Council. And whosoever taketh any of those that from this day forth accompany with him, shall have 5 marks for his reward truly to be paid in manner and form above said. And over this, commanding all constables, ministers, and officers of the said shire that none of them (on pain of death), take upon them to execute any commandment by word or writing sent or made unto them by the same Cade, calling himself Mortimer and Captain, be it to rear any people, or to any other intent; but to arrest and make to be arrested such as take upon them any such commandment by writing or by word.'

Appendix Five

The Act of Attainder 1450   29 Hen. VI. C.1

WHEREAS the false trator John Cade, naming himself John Mortimer, late named Captain of Kent, the VII day of July, the XXVIII year of the reign of our Sovereign Lord the King at Southwark, in the county of Surrey, and the IX day of July, the aforesaid year, at Deptford and Rochester in the county of Kent, also at the town of Rochester aforesaid and elsewhere, the X and XI of July then ensuing, within the Realm of England, falsely and traitorously imagined the King's defeat, Destruction and Subversion of this Realm, in gathering, and levying a great number of the King's people, and then exciting to make Insurrection against the King, at the Times before recited against the King's Royalty, Crown and Dignity; and there and then made and levied War falsely and traitorously against the King and his Highness. And though he be dead and mischieved, yet by the law of the land not punished. Our said Sovereign Lord the King, considering the Premises, to put such traitors in fear in time, and for the salvation of himself and of his realm, by advise of his Lords, Spiritual and Temporal in the said Parliament assembled, and at the request of his Commons, hath ordained by the authority of the said Parliament, That he shall be of these Treasons attainted, and that by the same authority he shall forfeit to the King all his goods, Lands and Tenements, Rents and Possessions, which he had the 8 day of July or after, and his Blood corrupt, and disabled for ever, and to be called a false Traitor within the said Realm for ever.

Appendix Six

The Act of Parliament making void all done under Cade's authority.   31 Hen. Vi.   1452-3

WHEREAS the most abominable Tyrant, horrible, odious and false Traitor John Cade, calling and naming himself sometime Captain of Kent, which name, Fame, Acts and Deeds to be removed out of the speech and mind of every man perpetually, falsely, and traitorously purposing and imagining the perpetual Destruction of the King's said Person, and final Subversion of this noble Realm, taking upon him Royal Power and gathereth to him the King's people in great number, by false subtil imagined language, and seditiously made a Commotion, Rebellion, and Insurrection, under colour of Justice, and Reform of the Laws of the said King, robbing, slaying, and spoiling great part of his faithful people; our said sovereign Lord the King considering the Premises, with many other which were more odious to remember, by Advice and Assent of the Lords aforesaid, and at the request of the said Commons, by the author aforesaid, hath ordained and established, That the said John Cade shall be reputed, named and declared a false Traitor to our said Sovereign Lord the King, and that all his Tyranny, Acts, Deeds and false opinions shall be voided, abated, annulled, destroyed and out of our Remembrance for ever; and that all the Indictments, and all Things depending thereof, had and made under the

Power of his Tyranny shall be likewise void, annulled, abated, repealed and holden for none; and that man's Blood be thereby defiled and corrupted, but by the Author of the said Parliament clearly declared for ever.

And that all Indictments in Time coming in like Case under Power of Tyranny, Rebellion and Commitment had, shall be of no Record nor Effect but void in law.

Appendix Seven

Chronological table of the events connected with the rising of Jack Cade. Not all these dates are exact

1445	Henry VI marries Margaret of Anjou.
1447	Duke of Gloucester dies.
1448–9	Normandy lost after serious English defeats. Rye and Winchelsea sacked and burned by the French.
Jan. 1450	Bishop of Chichester killed at Portsmouth. Suffolk impeached in Parliament.
March, 1450	Suffolk banished.
May, 1450	Suffolk intercepted and slain off Dover.
31.5.1450	Trinity Sunday. The insurgents assemble at Blackheath.
7.6.1450	The King and his army arrive in London. Negotiations with Cade produce Bill of Complaints and Requests.
16.6.1450	Cade retreats to Sevenoaks.
17.6.1450	King rides through streets of London.
18.6.1450	King and army reach Blackheath.
18–19.6.1450	Staffords attack Cade and are ignominiously defeated.
26.6.1450	Common Council of City of London dismissed.
29.6.1450	Cade reoccupies camp at Blackheath.

30.6.1450	Cade confers with King's envoys.
	King orders arrest of Lord Saye and retires to Berkampstead.
1.7.1450	Cade camps in Southwark and lodges at White Hart Inn.
3.7.1450	Common Council meet and decide to admit Cade.
	King departs for Kenilworth.
	Cade enters London, and strikes London Stone.
4.7.1450	Cade re-enters London and takes Crowmer for execution at Mile End.
	Contact of Cade's forces with forces from Essex.
	Cade compels Governor of Tower to hand over Lord Saye.
	Saye executed before his trial completed at Guildhall.
5.7.1450	Cade remains at Southwark.
	Londoners attack bridge at night.
6.7.1450	Battle goes on till 9.0 a.m. Truce then follows.
7.7.1450	Cade receives Archbishop of Canterbury, Cardinal Kempe and Bishop Waynflete. Pardons are granted and Bill of Complaints nominally accepted.
8.7.1450	Cade's forces begin to disperse.
9.7.1450	Cade marches on Deptford and Rochester.
11.7.1450	Cade attacks Queenborough Castle and is repelled.
12.7.1450	Cade takes flight and the rising ends.
	Government publish Proclamation for taking of Cade.
13.7.1450	Iden and his forces kill Cade at Heathfield.
16.7.1450	Cade's dead body beheaded and quartered and the quarters despatched to four towns.
1.8.1450	Commission of Assize opens in Kent.
9.11.1450	Act of Attainder passed against Cade.

Appendix Eight

Shakespeare on Jack Cade. Henry VI, Part II

Scene 2, Act IV

BEVIS: I tell thee, Jack Cade the clothier means to dress the commonwealth and turn it, and set a new map upon it.

———————

CADE: We, John Cade, so termed of our supposed father, for our enemies shall fall before us, inspired with the spirit of putting down kings and princes – Command silence! My father was a Mortimer. (*Dick:* He was an honest man and a good bricklayer.) My mother a Plantangenet. (*Dick.* I knew her well, she was a midwife.) My wife descended of the Lacies. (*Dick.* She was indeed, a pedlar's daughter and sold many laces. *Smith.* But now, of late, not able to travel with her furred pack, she washes bucks here at home.) Therefore am I of an honourable house. (*Dick.* Ay, by my faith, the field is honourable, and there was he born under a hedge – for his father had never a house but the cage.) Valiant I am. (*Smith.* 'A must needs; for beggary is valiant). I am able to endure much. (*Dick.* No question of that for I have seen him whipped three market days together). I fear neither sword nore fire. (*Dick.* But methinks he should stand in fear of fire, being burnt i' the hand for stealing of sheep.) Be brave then; for your captain is brave, and vows reformation. There shall be in England seven halfpenny loaves sold for a penny; the three-hooped pot shall have ten hoops; and I will make it felony to drink small beer; all the realm shall be in common; and in Cheapside shall my palfrey go to grass; and when I am king – as king I will be – there shall be no money; all shall eat and drink on my score; and I will apparel them all in one livery, that they may agree like brothers, and worship me their lord . . . Nay, that I mean to do. Is not this a lamentable thing, that of the skin of an innocent lamb should be made parchment, being scribbled o'er, should undo a man? Some say the bee stings; but I say 'tis the bee's wax, for I did but seal once to a thing, and I was never mine own man since.'

In the play Cade orders the execution of a clerk because he can write his name, and knights himself as Sir John Mortimer. Stafford declares that his father was a plasterer and Cade himself a shearman. Cade gives his pedigree, as expounded in earlier pages, but Stafford suggests that the Duke of York put him up to this, which Cade denies. Cade offers to protect Henry VI, but Dick announces that Saye's head is demanded because he sold the Dukedom of Maine.

CADE: And good reason, for thereby is England maimed, and fain to go without a staff, but that my puissance holds it up . . . he can speak French and therefore he is a traitor.

After declaring that his followers will be hung at their own doors, Cade says:

CADE: And you that love the commons follow me. Now show yourselves men: 'tis for liberty. We will not leave one lord, one gentleman; spare none but such as go in clouted shoon; for they are thrifty honest men, and such as would – but they dare not – take our parts.

After Cade has put on the armours of the dead Stafford, he says:

CADE: The bodies shall be dragged at my horse's heels till I do come to London, where we will have the Mayor's sword borne before us.

The Messenger who reports Cade's arrival to the King announces:

MESSENGER: The rebels are in Southwark; fly, my lord. Jack Cade proclaims himself Lord Mortimer, descended from the Duke of Clarence's house, and calls your grace usurper openly, and vows to crown himself in Westminster.

His army is a ragged multitude of hinds and peasants rude and merciless.

BUCKINGHAM: My gracious lord retire to Killingworth until a power be raised to put them down.

A second Messenger brings news of Cade's entry into London.

MESSENGER: Jack Cade hath gotten London Bridge. The citizens fly and forsake their houses. The rascal people, thirsting after prey join with the traitor, and they jointly swear to spoil the city and your royal court.

After Cade has entered London and performed the ceremony of London Stone, he says:

CADE: Now is Mortimer lord of this city; and here, sitting upon London Stone, I charge and command that, of the city's cost, the pissing conduit run nothing but claret wine this first year of our reign.

He adds that it is treason for anyone now to call him other than Lord Mortimer. A soldier crying: 'Jack Cade' is killed. Dick comes with news.

Dick . . . there's an army gathered together in Smithfield.

CADE: Come, then let's go fight with them, but first go and set London Bridge on fire and if you can, burn down the Tower too.

Dick petitions that the laws of England may come from Cade's mouth, while John remarks that Cade was thrust in the mouth with a spear and it is not whole yet. Smith adds that his breath stinks with eating toasted cheese. Cade later orders:

CADE: 'Burn all the records of the realm; my mouther shall be the Parliament of England' . . . 'and henceforward all things shall be in common.'

Cade, in a harangue to Lord Saye, complains that he gave up Normandy to Monsieur Basimecu,* the Dauphin of France. He includes among other crimes of this nobleman that he corrupted the youth of the realm in erecting a grammar school, caused printing to be used, and built a paper mill. He declares that the men about Saye talk of a noun and a verb and such abominable words as no Christian can endure, and that he appointed justices of peace and called poor men before them about matters they were not able to answer, and put them in prison, and because they could not read, hanged them.

Among other inaccuracies, Shakespeare gives 'Sir *James* Crowmer' as Saye's son-in-law.

CADE: There shall noe be a maid married vur she shall give him her maidenhead before they have it; men shall hold it of me in sapite; and we charge and command that their wives be as free as heart can wish or tongue can tell.

DICK: My lord, when shall we go to Cheapside and take up commodities upon our bills?

CADE: Marry, presently.

After the battle of the bridge, Buckingham with Lord Clifford and forces come to Cade as ambassadors from the King.

BUCKINGHAM: Know, Cade, we come ambassadors from the King unto the commons whom thou hast misled; and here pronounce free pardon to them all that will forsake thee and go home.

CLIFFORD: What say ye, countrymen? Will ye relent and yield to mercy whilst 'tis offer'd you; or let a rebel lead you to your deaths? Who loves the king and will embrace his pardon fling up his cap and Say God save his majesty! Who hateth him and honours not his father, Henry the Fifth, that made all France to quake, Shake he his weapon at us and pass by.

The peasants all cry; God save the King, and are rebuked

* The significance of this nickname is obvious

by their leader, whom they now say they will go on following. Clifford argues that the French are already taking advantage of the rebellion to attack. The multitude consequently recant, and declare their willingness to follow the king. Cade takes to flight and Buckingham offers 1,000 crowns as a reward for his capture.

Later, Cade's men are led to the king with halters about their necks, and Henry dismisses them to their own homes. Shakespeare's version of Cade's capture and death is recorded in the present text, but he ends the play with the statement that Iden drags his body by the heels to a dunghill, where he cuts off his head and takes it to the king, leaving the trunk for crows to feed upon. The King finally knights Iden.

The attentive reader of the facts set down earlier will appreciate the nonsensical quality of this account of the rising. Making full allowance for the necessity of representing it on a single stage and the limitations imposed upon the dramatist as a result; allowing also for dramatic licence; it is still easy to see that great liberties have been taken with the truth. The suggestion, for example, that Cade preached communism is unfounded.

Appendix Nine
Notes on Wat Tyler and the Peasant Rebellion

ONE

Uproar in England

[1]

WAT TYLER may have been, as has been suggested, a tiler by trade living in a Kentish town, but the greater likelihood is that he was an Essex man (from Colchester, perhaps). He enters recorded history on 7th June, 1381, in the lovely old town of Maidstone.

On this June day, the most conspicuous sight in Maidstone's handsome open market space was a milling mob of rough peasantry, gathered together in a state of uncertainty, but eager to be led, to have a strong hand over them, a sense of direction. They had come up the Medway from Rochester, where they had forced the Castle's Keeper, Sir John Newton, to surrender. They had set free prisoners there and liberated a man of their own kind who had, in their view, been unjustly imprisoned by a knight, Sir Simon Burley, whom they hated. These successes had given them confidence enough to loot and pillage what they could from the Castle. To the number of some thousands they swarmed into Maidstone on the sixth, and inspired more by emotion than reason, committed one outrage after another, until in the end they had blood on their hands. They had robbed a rich man, William Top-cliffe, of everything his house contained – to the value of 1,000 marks – equivalent to a fortune in our day. They had plundered and sacked wherever their fancy prompted them;

and now for some unexplained reason they finished up by murdering a burgess named John Southall, perhaps because he resisted their attack.

These peasants, uneducated, untrained in either politics or war, had become in a couple of days criminals whom the law would punish, if allowed to exist. There was but one course open to them: to destroy it; to continue their long march and remove the evil men and the evil regulations against whom and which they had risen. But they were like helpless sheep, not knowing what to do nor where to go. All passion temporarily spent, they needed someone to show them a goal and rekindle their rage. Such a man they found in Tyler.

In Dartford there is an old house claimed to be Wat's birthplace, but Tyler did not come from Dartford; not even, perhaps, from Maidstone. He was an unknown, as Cade was an unknown, but in essence he was everything Cade was not. Cade, either actually or by pretence, was a 'gentleman'. Tyler was never more than a rough boor, who had some remarkable qualities, it is true, but who sealed his own fate by his shortcomings. He seems to have been nothing more than a discharged soldier back from France, and there is a not unconvincing story that he was recognised by a Kentish man as a well-known rogue and highwayman. He never claimed to be of royal blood, and the revolt he headed owed nothing to him. He neither inspired nor created it. He merely rode upon the band-waggon, so to speak, after a prodigious leap that took him on to it. Throughout he showed neither the courtesy, the civility, nor the good sense of Cade. He had no statesmanship, no magnanimity. All he had was adroitness, ability to address a mob in words they understood and liked, a fair knowledge of military tactics, some cunning, a good deal of mistrust, and eventually, the lust for power that inevitably comes with its unbridled exercise.

The Chronicles of Froissart relate that Wat Tyler had once been a servant of Richard Lyons, an embezzler of public funds who had earned the abuse heaped upon him by Parliament. Lyons had been a high official under Edward III in France, and it was in Edward's wars that Tyler learned his soldier's trade. Because Tyler had once been beaten while in Lyons's service he treasured a grudge against him, which he remembered when the opportunity came.

The revolt led by Tyler was in its way a first rough impression, whereas Cade's was the finished job. Both risings started in Essex and Kent. Both found a leader in an unknown man. Both had considerable success at the start. Both camped at Blackheath. Both rebel armies entered London by way of a bridge left open for them. Both were on the brink of victory. Both failed by reason of temperamental shortcomings in their leaders. But having said this, one has said all. These are the points of similarity, but not the points of importance. The two risings were vastly different in origin, in scope, in leadership and in climax.

[2]

THE CADE REVOLT was essentially a rising of decent comfortable squires, gentry, merchants, traders, priests and countrymen against a Government that in their view was bringing the country to ruin. It had a multiplicity of grievances and a multiplicity of remedies. It was intensely vocal, orderly and efficient. The rising of Wat Tyler (or Teghler) – though as stated it was not in origin his rising at all – was much more a spontaneous upsurge of the desperate poor, tormented by a tax they resented, and inspired by the preaching of wandering friars to demand a better and more Christian way of life. They were not hungry, these men who surged up like an outbreak of smallpox in over twenty English counties; they wanted only freedom, decency, justice. They were sick of being treated as serfs by the lords of the manors; they were sick of having their pay settled for them irrevocably by Parliament; they were sick of monks and prelates every bit as ruthless as the lords in restricting the liberties of those who worked for them, who underpaid the parsons, and often took in tithes more than the parishes could afford.

Moreover, these men who revolted spontaneously and without co-ordination were better fed than they had been since the Black Death impoverished the country; they had been taught to believe in the Christian virtues of equality, compassion, humility, the value of each individual soul; they had learned to draw the long-bow, many of them, in the wars; to practise discipline; to respect themselves. They knew the value of good leadership in battle and that wars could be lost for the lack of it. And they had innumerable allies in the forests and woods, where there were companies, not exactly of 'partisans', as we have learned to call them, but of outlaws, thieves, men who had had their land stolen from them for some trivial offence, deer-stealers, tramps, beggars and wanted men.

Because it was widespread, this was at the outlet a much more dangerous revolt than Cade's. It was a Christian Communist outbreak. It expressed all the concentrated bitterness, the deep emotions, of Englishmen outraged by tyranny, misgovernment, corruption in high quarters, and heavy taxation. It had been brewing for a long time. It deserved a better fate and a better leader than it received.

What brought decades of discontent to a head was the notorious 'poll tax', decided upon by Parliament in the winter of 1380. The country was on the verge of bankruptcy. The last military expedition to France under Buckingham had cost so much for so little that writs were issued for a Parliament to meet in Northampton, which was considered safer than London. Money to continue the war was lacking; the customs duties had brought in much less than had been expected, owing to the loss of export duties on wool; even the King's jewels had been pawned; the armies in France were getting no pay; and money had had to be borrowed wherever a lender could be found.

Nobody suggested stopping the war. Instead it was decided to make every one of suitable age pay a tax of three groats a head. This tax was aimed particularly at the lower orders, because they were said to be getting all the advantages of national defence without contributing a penny towards it. It was, however, stipulated that the rich should help out the poor. In practice, however, in many rural localities the entire three groats (one shilling) had to be taken from the poorest inhabitants. It was only here and there that they paid as little as the original fourpence.

The wily peasant in virtually every locality 'wangled' his way out of the difficulty by faking his returns to the tax commissioners. Everyone knew this was being done, but no-one turned informer. Each village carefully left out of its returns all its widows, spinsters, aunts, daughters, and the non-earning women of its households. On paper the villages of England lost overnight most of their female population. For example, Kent, which returned 56,557 four years earlier, returned only 43,838 in 1381. In other words, 13,000 of the population had mysteriously disappeared in a period of rising population!

The Government were not slow to discover what was happening. They decided on 16th March not only to censure the local collectors and constables who had failed to check this evasion, but also to send out travelling commissioners who would go round in person and make sure that everyone who owed money paid it. In a short time they had uncovered instance after instance of fraud. Suffolk, for example, revealed 13,000 suppressed names!

Although beggars as usual were exempt from the poll tax, it had never before been the practice to extort cash from the poorest members of the community. It will be imagined, with what fury the hard-faced collectors were received when they presented themselves, not even accompanied by uni-

formed policemen or men-at-arms equipped for battle. They
trailed from one village to the next with perhaps a sergeant
or so, and a few petty pen-pushers to record their transactions, and made up for their obvious weakness by arrogance. Some of them may have behaved licentiously towards
the humble folk among whom they went. The legend that
Wat Tyler's daughter was molested and that this caused the
rebellion, may have had its foundation in some remembered
incident or incidents of the sort. Otherwise it is untrue.

The hatred they aroused, after simmering for months,
welled up in violence. Thomas Bampton, a recently appointed
commissioner, went on horseback into Brentwood, in Essex,
to look into the suspected false returns for the hundred of
Barstaple. When he came to examine the villages of Fobbing,
Corringham and Stanford, he discovered the fraud. He called
first the Fobbing men to meet him and pay what they owed.
They came, a small band of countrymen and men who lived
by fishing, and told him, in vulgar language, what he could
do with his demand. Not a penny more were they going to
pay. The inexperienced official, offended by such flagrant
disobedience and disrespect from a band of yokels, ordered
the pair of sergeants-at-arms to arrest the ringleader of this
resistance. The entire mass of marshlanders from Essex –
about a hundred in all – at once set about the half-dozen
officials, knocked them nearly senseless, and as they fled
back to London, flung stones at them, many of which found
their target.

The Government then sent Robert Belknap, a Chief
Justice of the Common Pleas, to bring these impertinent
fellows to justice.

[3]

THIS and not any eloquence of Wat Tyler, whose name at
that time was not even known or mentioned, was the spark

that lit the rebellion. As soon as Belknap reached Brentwood, escorted by only a handful of clerks, he was attacked by an armed mob, who arrested him, and putting before him a Bible, compelled him to swear that this was the last such commission on which he would ever sit. They tore up and burned his papers, murdered three of his clerks, beheaded a trio of local jurymen whose task should have been to name the chief offenders against Bampton, and with the heads of the dead men on the ends of long poles, marched in triumph through Brentwood, Fobbing, Corringham, and other villages, and having so easily overcome established authority, began to rob and ransack, to seethe and howl, throughout the whole of Essex. This period of uproar and rioting lasted for a week. There was no immediate reaction from London, and the feeling spread that nothing was to be lost by pressing victory to a conclusion. Moreover, as had been promised, a rising began in Kent under Abel Ker of Erith, who, after sacking a monastery at Lesness, crossed the Thames estuary for a conference with men of the Essex villages, and came back on June 4th with about a hundred of them.

This body, nothing like so numerous as the Essex contingent demonstrating around Brentwood, entered Dartford and harangued the populace there, urging revolt. Either shortly before or precisely at this moment, a judge and commission had arrived from London to look into the returns of the county of Kent. The judge was proceeding sedately on horseback towards Canterbury, where he was to set up his court, but before he could get there, he encountered a furious array of peasantry armed with bills and bows. They did not stone or beat him, as the Essex men had beaten and stoned Bampton, but sent him packing just as effectively.

By now all Kent was in ferment. Abel Ker was replaced as leader by a Dartford baker named Robert Cave, who gathered up the discontented from his own town, as well as from Erith, Bexley, Lesness and other minor centres, marched them to Rochester, and thence, as has been told, to Maidstone.

This, then, was the beginning of the unrest and anger that caught up Wat Tyler as by a great wave, and swept him to its crest.

TWO

The March on London

[1]

Two DAYS after Tyler's assumption of leadership, it was plain that the revolt was increasing in magnitude with every hour. Men were streaming in from villages for miles around to join the rebel force. Not only this, but fury was being vented in other ways. The mob had for years hated the royal officials, the men of law, the lords of the manors, and anyone connected in any way with John of Gaunt. They burned whatever official papers they could find, making great bonfires in the main streets of such towns as Dartford and Strood. They tore down a large manor house at North Cray, after robbing it of everything of value, and stole the cattle. They broke open the prisons, set free those they contained, and held four squires as hostages.

Two days were wasted thus, but in the end, Tyler established his authority sufficiently to give momentum and direction to the mob behind him. On the 10th June, the more disciplined and determined of his followers marched with him towards the great town of Canterbury. There was still no opposition from the Government, and none of a local kind. He was able, therefore, to march into Canterbury without shedding a drop of his army's blood, and because of this, the discontented of the town joined him in large numbers.

The difference between Cade and Tyler is exemplified

in the way they now behaved. Cade could have sacked Knole after his great victory over the King at Solefields. He left it alone. Tyler could have used Canterbury to strengthen his hold on England and disarm fear and suspicion. Instead, he proceeded at once to attack the Archbishop's palace.

Sudbury, the Archbishop, was the Chancellor and Prime Minister of Richard II, and was popularly blamed for the legislation to which the country had been subjected. In reality there is reason to suppose that he was neither a corrupt nor an insensitive man. He was sometimes tactless, sometimes weak, but his brief period of office – he was appointed in January 1380 – coincided unfortunately with the moment when social and political blunders attained their maximum effect. His victimisation by Tyler and his men was not in his capacity as Archbishop, but as statesman.

No mercy, no gentleness, no magnanimity, marked the entry of these gladiators. Sudbury was at his post in London, so could not be called to account in person. The local Sheriff, Sir William Septvans, was in the town, however, and an obvious target for the rebels. They did not kill him, but he was buffeted, bruised, and compelled to hand over for burning the records of which he was the custodian, so that many documents of the greatest possible interest to historians perished in the flames that scorched the cobblestones of the streets. The castle was entered and pillaged, and once more the prisons were emptied of their inhabitants, to the detriment of the moral stature of the rising.

Revolts encourage delation, and it is no credit to Tyler that it was encouraged. People were stopped in the street and asked to name any against whom they had grudges, and as 'traitors' such persons were seized and beheaded without trial, and probably without other justification than someone's personal hatred. Those not killed out of hand had their houses entered and their goods removed. Even their private papers, such as leases, bonds, etc., were burned. The local informers wanted all legal proofs of debts or obligations out of the way.

Although much damage was done to documents and houses, and a few people lost their lives, no excessive bloodshed took place. Indeed, considering the long-suppressed anger of the rebels, there was surprisingly little. Moreover, these men had the reverence for the Church and their religion characteristic of their time, and although on one occasion a band of them broke into a Canterbury cathedral service, their object seems only to have been to warn the monks to choose a new Archbishop, because when they got to London, Sudbury was going to be killed.

[2]

MORE DECISIVE in his movements than Cade, Tyler did not linger in Canterbury. After a day and night of looting and vengefulness, he began his rapid march on London, with the intention of taking it by storm and seizing the King before the Government could bring an army against him. Without waiting for accessions of strength from the rebels of more distant areas of Kent, he set off on the 11th and passed once more through Maidstone, where again there was the rioting and disorder that accompanied his arrivals at any town of size.

Tyler's march on London was rapid, occupying only two days, and as the army went, they were joined by companies from all the villages of west Kent. Nevertheless, their advance was not without incident. They found time to burst into the manor houses they passed and destroy the court-rolls or official documents. It was a singular feature of the rising that it was directed as much against the lawyers as against the squires and lords of the manor. Anything in the nature of a legal document appears to have been regarded as suspect and therefore fit only to be burned.

[3]

HERE we must note a remarkable difference between Cade and Tyler. Whereas Cade loitered at Blackheath for a week and then retreated to Sevenoaks, Tyler – a rougher, more decisive and coarser-thinking man – while bound to rest his men, saw the necessity of losing no time. He sent an advance force at once to Southwark and Lambeth. This was the signal for the restless, shifty population of those towns to rise in sympathy, while at the same time, men from the city of London who had crossed the river in boats, because the draw-bridge of London Bridge had been raised when it was known that Tyler was advancing, came flocking in to enlist under the rebel standard.

The first thing the advance party did was again to force the prisons and set free those within them. They then advanced a further couple of miles, and once more vented their anger, this time on the palace of the Archbishop, which they sacked at Lambeth. Here, too, they set fire to the house of John Imworth, Warden of the Marshalsea prison. It is said that the King himself, watching with his advisers in the Tower, could see the raging pillar of flame that lit the skies, while the unhappy citizens, staring out of their win-dows and from the upper floors of the offices and ware-houses over which they lived, could see figures silhouetted against the flames, and sparks eddying upwards across the river.

On the 11th June, the rebels set off again, and arrived next day at Mile End, where, as other rebels were to do nearly seventy years later, they camped in the open spaces, led by Thomas Farringdon of London, with Henry Baker of Manningtree, Adam Michel and John Starling. It is said that they came by arrangement with the men of Kent, but it is more probable that they learned of Tyler's advance, and wished to be in at the sack of London as soon as he. If there were to be pickings, they wanted their share.

So the 13th June dawned, with two rebel armies at the gates of London. Both bodies were highly satisfied with what they had so far achieved, and beyond doubt, the failure of the Government to oppose either advance had stimulated their spirits and confirmed their resolution. As night came and the flames flickered and died down, they slept content.

[4]

THE YOUNG KING RICHARD was a mere boy of fourteen. The only positive action that had been taken was the raising of the drawbridge to prevent the rebels from crossing London Bridge, and the closing of the gates all over the city. Guards had also been posted wherever important points had to be protected. That evening, June 12th, two meetings took place, one in the Tower, where the King and his council conferred, and the other in the Guildhall, where the Mayor, William Walworth, discussed with his Aldermen what should be done. Some of the troops that might have been got together to fight the rebels were on the high seas, having set off for Portugal under the Earl of Cambridge. A few about to embark for Brittany were recalled post-haste to London. In the city itself were only a few hired soldiers and archers under the command of Sir Robert Knolles, based on his own dwelling. There is no wonder the two meetings were attended by grave and worried men.

The militia were not called out because they could not be relied upon. The Government, taken by surprise, had no clue to the extent of the revolt. For all they knew, every man's hand was against them. That there were sympathisers in the population of the city was evident, since dozens had streamed across the river to join Tyler. (The upper classes have never been anxious to arm their subjects when their loyalty was doubtful.)

The truth of the matter is that not only were the Govern-

ment taken completely aback by the rising, but they had lost
their nerve. They were afraid, of the rebels, of their subjects,
even, perhaps, of each other, for in such moments there is
always the fear that one among them or more may be
planning to change sides.

Better than the King and his advisers the Mayor and
Aldermen knew the sullen resentment in the city; the angry
men among their own body who were ready to make a deal
with the rebels and use them to climb higher up the ladder.
Better than they, they knew the numbers who had crossed
over to Tyler or gone out into the districts to carry news of
the rebellion and foment local disturbances. What could be
done with so much uncertainty of power they did. In addition
to sealing off the bridge, they sent three Aldermen across the
river to Tyler's camp with a message.

These three were Adam Carlisle, John Frech and John
Horne (it is a coincidence that a later Horne was to play a
part in the Cade rebellion). The first two were loyal subjects
of the King, and as instructed, conveyed their message, to
the effect that Tyler and his men were to stay where they
were, and as soon as possible obey the King and go back to
their homes. The victorious marchers were probably in no
mood to listen to commands not backed up by obvious military
strength. But they had no need to weigh the consequences of
disobedience. Horne was one of those who had made up their
minds that a change of government was necessary. Behind the
backs of his companions, he saw Tyler in secret, and explained
to him and his lieutenants that all London was prepared to
support him. If he advanced towards the bridge, he could rely
upon the Londoners to see that the way was made easy.

This was precisely the news Tyler hoped to hear, and that
Cade, years later, was to wait for in vain. Three of Tyler's
chief men slipped across the river with Horne and hid in his
house in the city. As soon as it was safe to walk abroad, Horne
took them to the meeting-places of those who sympathised
with the revolt, and there plans were drawn up for the follow-

ing day. Somehow a messenger was sent back to the rebel camp with news that convinced Tyler his capture of the city was imminent. Horne, who had at least the courage of his convictions, now took the extraordinary step of approaching Walworth, the Mayor, and insisting that no risk whatsoever would be run if Tyler was allowed to enter the city without opposition. This, he said, was the surest way of preventing the enraged men from doing to the houses and palaces what they had done elsewhere. What the Mayor replied is not known.

But the King and his Council had not been totally idle. Like the Mayor, they too, had sent an envoy to Tyler, inquiring what his motives were in marching on the city, and had received the reply that the rebels had no quarrel with Richard; they were prepared to remain his loyal subjects; but they had a care for the name of their native land, and had in mind only to put their complaints to him. Their quarrel was with John of Gaunt and other ministers, who in their opinion had brought their country near to ruin.

When this reply came, Sudbury, the Archbishop, and the Treasurer of the land, Sir Robert Hales, wished to ignore it. Richard, however, in striking contrast to the frightened Henry VI of Cade's day, had courage and will. He wanted to hear for himself what these furious men had to say, and therefore notified the insurgents that he was coming across the river to meet them. He chose as the meeting-place a part of the river bank below Blackheath. It was early in the morning, and the rebels prepared to receive their royal guest.

THREE

London at His Feet

[1]

THE SCENE on that June morning, with a chill in the air and a
hint of mist still rising from the surface of the river, must have
been impressive. All along the sloping shore of the river there
stood a mass of armed men, to the number, it is estimated, of
ten thousand. Suddenly, where the Tower of London lifted
its proud walls, a glitter and stir showed that a barge was
being launched. With a shout of joy, the rebels saw the heavy,
ornamented barge with the King and his companions leave
the north bank and sail down the river towards Greenwich.
With the King were the Chancellor – Archbishop Sudbury,
the Earls of Warwick, Salisbury and Oxford, and a number
of councillors. Four smaller craft followed in the wake of the
king's.

In what followed, it is possible to discern the vast difference
between the orderly army of Cade and the army of Tyler.
Tyler, whatever influence he had when directing a march or
an attack, had no such control over his men as the later leader.
No sooner was it seen that the King was unquestionably
coming over to confer than all discipline was lost. The decent
countrymen among them cheered their monarch fervently,
but as many, if not more, burst into frenzied howls, clamour-
ing for the deaths of John of Gaunt and the wretched
Chancellor, waved their weapons wildly, and behaved like the

hooligans many of them were. What confronted the King as he drew near the south bank was not a body of leaders in command of orderly ranks, but a mob, lusting for violence, screaming, yelling, uncontrolled and uncontrollable.

All idea of landing was abandoned. The most that could be done was to draw sufficiently near for the King's voice to carry. Pandemonium increased until, about eighty yards from the landing place, the rowers ceased to move their blades and the barge came to a halt. For a few moments surprise stilled the howls and clamour, and during this fortuitous pause, Richard was able to address the multitude. What he said in effect was: 'Here I am. Tell me what you want.'

The mob began to snarl and shout again, insisting that before they would talk to him, he must come on shore. Even the brave young King was not such a fool as to risk his royal person among so brawling and insolent a mass of louts. Sudbury, whose blood had been demanded, would certainly have been torn to pieces had he landed, and the King would not endanger the lives of his ministers. Moreover, it was plain that once the rebels had him in their midst, they would hold him both as hostage and as puppet to do their will.

He appears, however, to have hesitated, because the records aver that not he gave the order to the rowers to go back to the Tower, but Sudbury himself or the Earl of Salisbury. The clumsy, gilded barge began to draw away from the south bank.

To see the King escape from their hands must have been infuriating to the assembled soldiers. They swore, raged, cursed, rushed up and down flinging cries of 'Treason!' after the royal party. Only one fanatic with a longbow was needed to shoot an arrow into the King, which would have been the signal for a hail of other arrows to destroy the entire party. That the King and his companions reached the northern shore unharmed suggests that for all their noise and savagery,

O

there was none in the rebel army eager or prepared to commit the sin of regicide.

[2]

THE INSURGENTS now determined to capture London. They were beginning to run short of supplies, and if they had been denied entry, they might have had to disperse. This, however, is not proved.

The men of Blackheath now set off not, like Cade, in retreat, but towards their advance guard at Southwark. By now, Alderman John Horne had once more crossed the bridge, and was there to meet them, carrying a royal standard, and mounted on a horse. As the rebels streamed into the town and towards the bridge – there is no hint that at any time they marched with precision in proper formation – Horne urged them to go forward over the bridge, promising they would meet no opposition. This was no idle word, because at this precise moment one of Horne's supporters, Alderman Walter Sibley (or Sybyle) of Billingsgate was preparing to let them in.

This bold and daring rascal was apparently in charge of the Southwark end of the drawbridge, accompanied by a small number of troops, and when offered the assistance of some armed citizens of standing in the city, he summarily dismissed them, saying he was quite capable of looking after the district for which, as an alderman, he was responsible, and that they would do better to go back and see to their own affairs. This they did, no doubt disgusted and indignant at their treatment, and the cunning Alderman settled down to await events.

These were not long delayed. Encouraged by Horne's harangue, the rebels, howling and rampaging, came hurrying towards the drawbridge. The moment they appeared, Sibley cried out that a handful of soldiers could not hope to overcome so vast an array, and ordered his subordinates to lower the drawbridge. This was done, and at once the rebel army rushed across London Bridge and set foot on the northern shore.

Here they should have met closed gates and armed resistance, but yet another Alderman, whose motives have been variously interpreted, opened Aldgate to them, and as no preparations had been made to oppose the entering army, it was not long before Tyler was master of the city.

The worst had happened. There, on the citizens' doorsteps, was this ferocious horde, whose behaviour was unpredictable, under the leadership of a rough soldier whose methods gave little hope of scrupulous and restrained action. The terrified loyal citizens hid in their houses, barring the doors. The more important and more obviously threatened took refuge in the Tower. But as always, there were large numbers who had no great attachment to either King or rebels, and sought to ensure their own safety by welcoming the Kentish men. They trundled out great tuns of ale and tapped them for the newcomers, besides offering provisions and refreshment.

As with the opening days of the Cade entry into London, the rebels at first behaved correctly, and did no damage. A few even paid for what they ate and drank. The importance of retaining the goodwill of the city was plain to Tyler and his lieutenants, and the impression is gathered that for once they had taken control of their followers, who were told repeatedly that they must not forget their primary purpose, which was to punish John of Gaunt, Archbishop Sudbury, Sir Robert Hales, and other leading men of Richard II's entourage.

It must have been galling to Tyler that these intended victims were safely out of harm's way in the Tower, and in his anger, he gave his men leave to attack the splendid residence of John of Gaunt, the Savoy, said to be the handsomest in the whole realm of England. The men, now fed, and slightly if not wholly intoxicated after copious free ale, did not need much prompting. The London men, eager to placate these ruffians, took the lead and showed them which way to go. They poured bawling and roaring into the Strand, announcing their destination at the tops of their voices.

It was now four in the afternoon, and the soldiers had collected up willy-nilly as they went all the riff-raff of a city, out for pickings.

[3]

THE CONTROL exercised by Tyler and his officers over their men that day had not yet broken down. The attack on the Savoy palace was not a brutal, barbarous massacre preceded by armed robbery. Instead, it was a systematic annihilation of valuable property. The smashing in of the doors led to ordered and complete destruction of everything the building contained. The textiles were hacked and tattered until they were merely fragments littering the floors. The handsome furniture was tossed out into the street and smashed to matchwood by the mob. There was no opposition from within. If John of Gaunt had left servants to guard his house, they had vanished. Everything that could be broken into pieces, however precious and beautiful, was pounded with hammers and thrown into the Thames. Jewels were reduced to powder and the carpets ripped into shreds.

When nothing remained but mutilated remnants, three barrels of gunpowder were brought and fired, and the entire building, flaming to the heavens, went down in complete and final ruin. This was vandalism, insensate vengefulness, the work of petty men, not of great reformers or idealists. This act in itself gives the quality of Wat Tyler. The one redeeming fact is that there was no looting. It was destruction, not robbery, and when a hanger-on was seen scuttling away with a silver cup, he was immediately arrested and executed.

Nevertheless, while discipline was preserved by the armed men, they could not and did not prevent the wilder elements from penetrating into the wine-cellars, where they made merry with the contents, and finished up drunk and immovable on the stone flags. They were still there when the flames broke out, and from those cold black depths they never again emerged.

We shall never know whether what happened next was desired by Tyler or not. If it was, then it was in keeping with his general behaviour. If not, then it indicates how little significance his leadership had. However this may be, the next few hours were spent in a perfect orgy of destruction. The church of the Temple was raided, and every book the massive chests contained was gutted and put on another bonfire in the street. (There were precedents in history for the Nazi burning of the books.) The Inns of Court themselves were penetrated, and wanton damage done. First, every chest, cupboard or container was demolished and flung into the street to make firewood, and then the charters, parchments, records, papers, books, were slashed, ripped, torn, and tossed into the flames. The fodder of history was consumed by these heedless, ignorant asses.

All London succumbed to a vast paralysis of fear. Not a protest was heard, not a hand raised itself in fury against these rustic Goths. The men of law and those who sat at their feet had gone running off, even the old and weak, as quickly as their legs could carry them. There were no bands of townsfolk flocking to defend these relics, to safeguard their town against further outrage. London lay at Wat Tyler's feet, and those feet were not yet still. Clumsy, careless, they stamped and trampled even during the hours of darkness.

Even the sacking of the Temple had not sated these brutal men. They surged into Clerkenwell, headed by Thomas Farringdon, on horseback. This man, though himself a Londoner, had been instrumental in goading the Essex men into revolt, and was now riding before them as their leader. Here the Priory of St John's, where Hales lived, was ransacked and consumed by fire, while the hospital and the house of the Hospitallers were also destroyed. A number of

Flemings, taken by surprise, had rushed into the church and claimed sanctuary at the altar, but this did not save them. They were torn from the body of the church, taken out and put to death.

By this time, darkness had come down, but still the cruel work went on. The prisons of the Fleet and Newgate were broken into and destroyed, the prisoners being released. A number of citizens' dwellings in Holborn were left in ruins. Fire, burglary, murder, were but incidents of that dreadful day. Over and above the seven Flemings killed, nine other men were murdered, including Roger Legett, who had taken sanctuary in St Martin's-le-Grand, and was whisked away to Cheapside, where the executioner with his axe ended his life. The released prisoners undoubtedly performed many of these dreadful acts, but this does not excuse the leaders. Many crimes were committed by the rats of London during Cade's occupation of the city, but these men came out only after the leader and his men had gone back to their camp in Southwark. Wat Tyler and his officers were there, on the spot, in broad daylight. They knew what was being done in their name, and could have stopped it with a shower of arrows or a brandishing of swords. They made no attempt to do so. We must presume that they looked on, helplessly or with grim satisfaction, or participated.

There came a time when even these men wearied. As the last fires burned, the last charred flakes drifted up and away from the glowing ashes in the streets, as the last victim screamed his protests, the mob sought sleep, some in the alleys from which they had come; some in dingy garrets where they had been offered or found shelter; but mostly they camped on the flat stretches of Tower Hill and St Catherine's wharf. Here they built great fires by whose light their sentries could see movements to or from the Tower, which they now ringed with steel. This ring the monarch would have to break if he wished to retain his crown.

FOUR

The King Parleys

[1]

THE ARMY SLEPT, but Tyler and his lieutenants were wide awake. In the dead of night they betook themselves to Farringdon's London abode, and there considered their course of action for the following day. It is said that they drew up a list of men they intended to execute, among whom were John of Gaunt, Sudbury the Archbishop, John Fordham, Clerk of the Privy Seal and Bishop-Elect of Durham, Chief Justice Belknap, Chief Baron Plessington, Sir Ralph Ferrers, John Legge, who was believed to have been the originator of the poll-tax commissioners, Thomas Bampton and Sir Thomas Orgrance, Hales's second-in-command as Treasurer. It is curious that Hales himself is missing from this list. The rebels may have believed him out of London.

These new masters of the city were not the only wakeful ones on that surly night. Away in the Tower, glimmering still with the light from the fires of the Strand and Clerkenwell, another meeting was taking place. Haggard, red-eyed, the boy-King and his ministers were debating. Now and again, a roystering band of soldiers, returning from some foray of destruction and not yet lost in sleep, howled insults at the Tower walls, vowing to storm it next day and crying for the blood of the 'traitors' they knew to be within. Wherever the ministers looked they were surrounded. By fear and panic they had been prevented from taking even elementary precautions against siege and imprisonment. They had made no plans to bring in loyal forces from the country. They had been cut off from escape by the treachery that had yielded London to Tyler long before it had seemed possible.

The opinions expressed at this conference were widely different. One argument was that a surprise night attack should be made while most of the insurgents were sleeping. If a well-armed body of men could cut through the ring, they could quickly rally sufficient men from the city itself to hack the rebels to pieces. This argument came from the loyal and spirited Mayor; but he had a redoubtable opponent. The Earl of Salisbury was convinced that such a harebrained scheme was bound to fail. A trained soldier, he claimed to know what he was talking about. It might be possible for brave fighters to take advantage of darkness and surprise. They might even get through the circle and break out into the streets; but the besiegers were numerous, and there were, it was obvious, so many malignant and unprincipled ruffians from the city slums at Tyler's disposal that it might prove impossible to unite even with such loyal men as came forward to join their King and his army. Darkness, which undoubtedly would aid a surprise attack, would be a handicap to the continuance of the operation. It would be difficult to mass, to manoeuvre, in the narrow streets, where daggers might strike undetected from the shadows. Friend could not be distinguished from foe.

In short, if the attack failed, they might all be broken into small bodies fighting desperately without a plan of campaign, and complete defeat must follow. Then the King would be in greater danger than before, and there was no knowing what might become of him and them. Improvisation was all very well, but unless there was a planned follow-through, it was best avoided.

Salisbury emerged victor of the debate, and steps were at once taken to implement his proposals. A couple of knights were despatched by the King under a flag of truce, with a request in writing that the rebels should put down on paper what they wished the King to do, choose a deputation to bring this answer to him, and then go home, relying on the honour of the King to see that justice was done. The two knights made their way to St Catherine's Wharf, where they were brought before an assembly of soldiers roused from sleep. Torches threw a reddish glare on their faces, and a battered old chair was dragged from some resting-place. On this one of the envoys stood, and by torchlight read out the words the King had written.

The stratagem was not subtle enough to deceive men who had learned by bitter experience to distrust written documents and the false words of the mighty. They told the knights to go back inside and not come out again until they had a better message. The discomfited emissaries returned and reported the poor reception they had had.

The weary Councillors embarked upon a fresh discussion, and in the end agreed that on the following morning the King in person should concede to Tyler and his men the face-to-face encounter that he had refused to grant them when they came to Blackheath and had not been able to grant at Southwark.

Richard, instead of being stricken by fear, accepted this plan with enthusiasm. He was convinced he had only to talk to his people and they would listen to him. He wanted the meeting as soon as ever it could be arranged, and *commanded* the rebels to meet him in the meadows at Mile End between seven and eight the following morning – Friday. There was more in the choice of Mile End than met the eye. The area was well-known and liked in those days as a place for strolling in leisure hours. To attend the meeting with the King, the insurgents would have to pass out through the city gates, and if enough did so, it might be possible to shut them out, and keep them there. If this proved impracticable, at least the ring round the fortress would be broken, and some of the more notable refugees, such as Sudbury and Hales, could remove themselves from danger.

The letter was delivered to the multitude besieging the Tower, and no time was lost by them in agreeing to attend the proposed meeting. It looked as if Salisbury's advice had been good, and in this hope and belief, a few hours of sleep were snatched by both sides.

[2]

FRIDAY DAWNED, and the King rose early. The first news brought to him was bad. Tyler had not been negligent. Either because he suspected trickery or because he was a capable soldier, he had moved most of his forces outside the city gates, but had left enough well-equipped and mettlesome men behind to keep a close watch on the Tower. In the early hours, when a boat had carried the escaping Sudbury as far as the water-gate and a little beyond, he had been perceived, and compelled to abandon his attempt.

Nevertheless, Richard kept his appointment. It was approximately seven o'clock when he and his companions rode out of the Tower, though the two who had most to fear, Sudbury and Hales, were missing. The sight of these hated men within their very grasp might have been too much for the rebels. However, sufficient soldiers were left in the Tower to prevent its capture by a surprise attack, and only a handful of councillors followed their King.

The danger to the King lay not only in voluntarily placing himself within reach of the rebels but also in making his way through the streets. It is related, indeed, that on Tower Hill, the same Thomas Farringdon whose house had sheltered Tyler and whose tongue had incited Essex to revolt, rushed forward, took hold of the bridle rein of the King's horse, and shouted out a rough demand for justice.

Richard did not lose either his head or his temper. He

replied with extraordinary sagacity that Farringdon should get what he was justly entitled to. Farringdon then let go of the horse, but was not content with this evasive answer. Instead of going on to Mile End, he gathered a handful of his Essex men together, and slyly made his way to the Tower, in the hope of himself capturing Hales, whom he must now have discovered to be there.

Hardly was this incident over when the previous Mayor of London, Nicholas Bramber, had his horse pulled up sharply by a commoner named William Trewman, who flung insults at him and had to be forcibly stopped from a direct assault. Throughout the entire journey the horsemen and their monarch had to move through a howling, resentful crowd of sightseers, eager for mischief, yet even now not daring to profane the royal person.

Towards the fields of Mile End there came a diminution of the mob, and a gap appeared through which, as quietly as they could, two of the King's retinue, the Earl of Kent and Sir John Holland, turned their horses and slid away. Once clear, they made off at a fast pace to the meadows beyond Whitechapel. This was an act of treachery that can be neither excused nor forgotten, for these two men were half-brothers of the King. It is a tribute to Richard that at a later date, he pardoned them.

Despite all disturbances and risks, the King arrived safely in the fields of Mile End.

[3]

THERE WAS HERE no secret conference in a tent, such as Cade later afforded to Henry's envoys at Southwark. This was public debate in the open air, with all its drawbacks and interruptions, its half-finished sentences and brusque catcalls, its heckling and mindless gibbering. The initiative appears to have been taken by Tyler himself, who concentrated primarily on his demand that the virtual serfdom of the peasants should be abolished. He wanted all lands to be leased at a flat yearly rate of fourpence an acre. This is important, because it focussed attention in later years on this state of feudal serfdom, and may be said to have been the first nail in its coffin.

Richard had been well-primed by his advisers. He could not afford to hedge or palter.

Whether sincere or not, he promised to get rid of serfdom, to adopt the rent of fourpence an acre for land tenanted by the villeins, do away with whatever regulations stopped the countryfolk from marketing and buying as they wished, and prevent any particular locality from having a monopoly of the market. He also promised that if the rebels went home without further offence, they would be given a general amnesty to cover whatever crimes they had committed since they left their homes. As a token of this he would give each band a royal standard and finally he undertook to put a body of thirty clerical men to work preparing the necessary charters, which each rebellious locality would come forward to collect. That these charters were actually drawn up is proved, and their wording can be read in the chronicles today by those interested.

Tyler was shrewd and naturally suspicious. The King had uttered not a word concerning one of the most important of all the demands he and his men had come to London to enforce. There were men about the King whom the rebels were not prepared to tolerate. Tyler was quick to detect the King's failure to mention these ministers and officials. He insisted that they must be arrested and probably executed, since the word he used to describe them – traitors – implied death as the penalty. Richard stuck to his original promise. Anyone proved in open and fair trial to have betrayed his King and country, should be arrested, and if guilty, have justice done to him.

Having said this, he continued to address the mob,

repeating his fair words, and handing out the standards and banners promised to those who claimed amnesty for their offences. Tyler, feigning acceptance of these offers, withdrew with his assistants into the background. All seemed well, and no doubt the beating hearts of the King's companions slowed as he moved about unassailed.

But they would have been less confident had they seen a small band of horsemen and men-at-arms with Tyler leading gallop quietly from the Mile End fields and into London by the open gate, heading straight for the Tower. Altogether, a few hundreds came riding up to the fortress that June morning. There must linger in the minds of any who read the account of this seemingly wild ride, the suspicion that it was made with foreknowledge. When Tyler reached the Tower, he found no portcullis down, no drawbridge raised. The officer and soldiers at the gate offered no resistance. The insurgents were able to ride straight over the bridge into the fortress itself, and to go about among the guards, pulling their whiskers in fun, joking, expressing fraternity with them both then and for the future, avowing their leader's intention not to harm them, but to wreak vengeance on the 'traitors', those rascals hiding in the precincts. This was the behaviour of men sure of the guards' complicity, not of men moving by force among hostile troops.

Once past the sentries, the insurgents split up traversing the entire Tower in search of their enemies. Side by side with Tyler was the ever-present Essex ringleader, Thomas Farringdon. They were not assailed or impeded by the soldiers quartered there, even when they burst into the King's own bedroom and searched the bed in case a 'traitor' lay hidden beneath it, even when the Princess of Wales in her private apartment was again assailed by rough men breaking in upon her, one of whom, according to Froissart, attempted to embrace her; even when the wanted men were found and dragged to their doom.

The Princess of Wales had collapsed and become unconscious at this new incursion, and her pages, as soon as the rebels had departed, carried her to a boat and succeeded in conveying her to the 'Queen's Wardrobe', a house in the Tower Royal near St Paul's cathedral. Meantime, the titled men and 'gentlemen' looked on.

Archbishop Sudbury had retreated, after the failure of his attempt to escape, to the Tower chapel, where he performed his devotions, confessed his sins, and communicated the prior-treasurer (Hales) whose death could also be expected if the mob laid hands upon him. Both men passed the long hours after the King's departure for Mile End in singing, chanting, intoning. It is written that the Archbishop had come to the words *omnes sancti orate pro nobis* when the door burst open and the savages rushed in, shrieking with joy at sight of their prey.

Sudbury had courage. He neither cringed not held his tongue, but moved boldly forward, declared himself the Archbishop, and denied either treason or deliberate oppression of the poor. His courage did him no service. He was seized, beaten, torn from the chapel, and hurried through the Tower yards to the hill, where a log of wood was made the pillow for his head, and a clumsy, amateur headsman needed eight strokes to sever skull from trunk. Hales had been taken at the same time as Sudbury, and his head rolled soon afterwards. Two other victims, a Franciscan friar named William Appleton, and John Legge, the advocate of the poll-tax, were put to death in the same place and in the same manner. The four severed heads were, in the horrible ritual of the time, impaled on long poles and carried about the streets, after which they decorated the gate of London Bridge.

The rebels now made a serious tactical error. Having the Tower in their hands, they did not disarm its defenders, take possession, and create a virtually impregnable centre on which to pivot and manoeuvre. They did not even spike the guns. Instead, they left the fortress and did not forbid the guard to shut the gates behind them. This was as great a blunder as Cade's, when he refrained from an all-out attack on the Tower, and shows clearly that while Tyler was a good soldier in small actions, he had no strategy, no overall conception of how to turn a military advantage to account.

When he turned his back on the fortified Tower and headed for the city, Tyler ended whatever hope he might have had of becoming England's master.

FIVE

End of an Adventurer

[1]

THE KING, learning that the Tower was taken, had no desire to place himself at the mercy of a man who, powerless while the common folk stayed awe-stricken before their monarch, would have no scruples when that monarch was securely locked in a cell. Leaving behind a trustful and cheering people, he went by way of Aldgate to where his mother, the Princess of Wales, lay at the 'Wardrobe'.

With him there travelled a deputation from the peasants entrusted with the task of receiving all the remaining charters that the clerks were still copying. The afternoon was passed in this work, and the documents were handed to the representatives of the various bands, particularly those from Essex. When the deputation returned bearing these precious documents, they were greeted enthusiastically; and firmly convinced that their King's word was as good as law, the more credulous and least politically-minded began to leave Mile End and start the journey back to their private hearths, believing they had achieved all they had come to do.

But these were a proportion only of those who constituted the rising, and as many as thirty thousand men remained under Tyler without claiming charters from the King. They had other fish to fry. London was theirs, they believed, and there was much to be done.

This day, 14th June, Friday, 1381, was one of the most horrible in English history, making an orgy of malevolence, an outburst of cruelty, hate and violence, such as few eras before our own have seen. All pretence that the rebels were eager to eliminate the 'traitors' only vanished, and the entire force, together with its sordid allies from the slums, began a long day of murder, arson and brutality. Foreigners were the first target. There had always been resentment among the Londoners at the existence and prosperity among them of the Flemings and Lombards, who corresponded at that time to the Jews in Nazi Germany. It was openly announced that anyone who wished could kill any Fleming or other foreigner he came across, and this permission applied not merely to Tyler's own men, but to any citizen of London.

Between noon and midnight something like 150 or 160 foreigners were beheaded or killed in other ways. Sometimes men were picked out as they walked inoffensively through the streets, asked to pronounce some difficult English word, and if their tongues or accents were not what the attackers were accustomed to, immediately executed. The Lombards were perhaps less frequently murdered than the Flemings, of whom 35 were slain in a single body after being snatched from St Martin in the Vintry, but their homes were pillaged and fired.

Anyone whom Tyler and his men disliked was killed. There was no question, here, as with Cade, of slum-dwellers getting out of hand when the rebel army had gone. This was Tyler, a Hitler of his day, at work in person. He hunted Richard Lyons until he found him, and beheaded him on the spot in revenge for the blows this man when his master had inflicted upon him. John Greenfield was slain in Cheapside for declaring that Friar Appleton had been executed for no good reason. Howling mobs went about the town challenging everyone to state their allegiance, and if the man interrogated did not answer 'King Richard and the true commons', he was assaulted, carried by force to one of the logs that

P

had been placed at every road intersection, and his head cut off.

Lawyers, jurymen, tax-collectors and commissioners, Lancastrian partymen, were all victims of this wild and reckless slaughter. But before long even the frail structure of political and social grievance collapsed, and there reigned naked spite. Those with grudges and envies flung their enemies before the murderers with lying accusations and saw them killed.

One ruffian, Jack Straw, set fire to the manor house of the Prior of St John at Highbury. Another burned John Butterwick's house at Knightsbridge, then a pleasant little village. In London itself, Alderman Horne, who, with his confederate, had opened London Bridge to the rebels, was a great man in his own estimation as he rode up and down the streets followed by a swarm of riff-raff, forcing men to abandon their homes on the pretext that they occupied them unlawfully; compelling men to give up to those who owed money the notes of hand given; fining any person whom he took to be a money-lender or an embezzler. Even priests and elderly women were forced to surrender their paltry pence. This was mob-rule and revolt gone mad.

[2]

THE KING, throughout this diabolical uproar, was still sheltering in the 'Wardrobe', which was in no way capable of resisting an attack. It is doubtful if Tyler knew or cared now where he was.

As with the Nazis in World War II, however, early success followed by insensate cruelty and brutality produced their inevitable reaction. The decent Londoners saw for the first time, perhaps, that nothing good could be expected from men who behaved like this. They began to bolt and bar their houses, take out their arms, get ready to oppose entry and if

necessary, fight to save their wives, children and possessions.
A drunken crowd rushing for the Guildhall to destroy all the
precious books and legal parchments it contained found the
strong oaken doors shut in their faces, and no hammering and
shouting persuaded those within to open.

Nevertheless, these desperate reactions were individual,
unco-ordinated. The long night dragged on, and under cover
of darkness apprentices are said to have killed their masters,
debtors their creditors, lovers their mistresses' husbands, and
heirs their fathers.

Nor, when dawn came on the Saturday, 14th June, was
there much change for the better. The Marshal of the Marshalsea Prison, John Imworth, who had fled for sanctuary to
Westminster Abbey, and who was kneeling with his arms
about the marble pillar of Edward the Confessor's shrine,
was caught by a mob, invading the abbey, who had no regard
for tradition and no reverence for the church. They beheaded
him at Cheapside. The King sent yet another envoy to suggest
that as the rebels seemed dissatisfied with what he had
already given and promised them, they should meet him for a
second time outside Aldersgate, in the wide spaces of
Smithfield.

This was dangerous. The insurgents had now gone into
such deep waters they knew there would be no hope of
rescue. The better men among them had begun their long
journey home, and Richard was left to face a rabid mass of
released convicts, fanatical adventurers, sly rogues eager for
power, and twisted characters without loyalty, respect or
reverence. Nevertheless, it was no more dangerous than
waiting supine. There was no doubting now that Tyler was
a mad dog. He had gone about the previous evening swearing
that he and his twenty thousand men would behead anyone
who lifted a hand against him, and that at the end of four more
days he would be England's lawgiver. (Never once did Cade
utter so crude and violent a sentence.) It was plain that unless
he were stopped now, he would soon be England's king. Only

the magic of the King's presence and the cunning of his advisers could prevent this from happening.

Although bursting with satisfaction at the commotion he had caused and the destruction he had created, Tyler still doubted his authority over Richard. He agreed to meet him.

The Council and high personages with Richard had not deserted him, other than the two already named. When the news came that Tyler had agreed to the meeting, the solemnity of the occasion came over them. They undoubtedly felt that everything had been put into the scales and only the Lord could decide the result. They rode all the way to Westminster to take the sacrament before the high altar. The King absented himself for a short time, and confessing to an anchorite he found there, received absolution.

The rest prayed at the shrine of Edward the Confessor, and then, as the minutes ticked by and the time came for departure, the King returned. They set off for Smithfield, a compact body of some two hundred armed horsemen, with armour beneath their cloaks or robes.

Unmolested, the royal company arrived and found Tyler and his men awaiting him. They pulled up their horses and stood, silent, before the church of St Bartholomew, to the east of the open space. Tyler and his men were this time drawn up in proper formation on the western side. There was a kind of no-man's land between the two groups. For a time they faced one another in silence, each waiting for the other to make the first move. It was like toreador facing bull, with the assembly watching and hushed.

[3]

IT WAS THE KING who acted. He caused Walworth, the Mayor, to announce that he would hear from their own leader what new requests they had to make. Tyler interpreted this as a signal to him to demonstrate his dominance. Though seated on only a small workaday horse, he moved into the open space, accompanied by one other man, carrying his banner. Then, little knowing what he was doing, he took the steps that ended all his mastery. Dismounting, out of genuine or feigned respect for his King, he moved forward, made obeisance, took the royal hand in his, and grasped it warmly.

With this gesture of friendship and reverence, he began by declaring that inside a couple of weeks the King would be even more esteemed by the common people of England than he already was for his generous action in coming to meet them. Concealing any repugnance he felt at the plebeian touch and the patronising words, Richard asked bluntly why he and his men had not gone home, everything they demanded at their first meeting having been granted to them.

Tyler replied that the changes still to be made were much more fundamental and far-reaching. The only law of the land should be that of Winchester (referring presumably to a Statute drawn up in the reign of Edward I). The lords were to have their claws cut and be given less power. The rich estates owned by the church should become the property of the state, with compensation for the existing holders, and be carved up among the people. There should be only one bishopric. Men should be free and equal before the law, with the sole exception of the King.

These demands could not be conceded without long discussion. To argue them out in the open air in the presence of an ignorant horde of swashbuckling rascals was impossible. Richard's reply was inevitably equivocal. He replied that he would agree to those demands the law of the land allowed him to grant, apart from matters affecting his own kingship. This answer revealed that the whole matter would, in the royal opinion, have to be submitted to Parliament, and that the King would not take upon himself to grant there and then these ridiculous demands.

During these pregnant minutes, while Tyler slowly grasped that what he had elicited was, in effect, a refusal, not a sound was heard. No-one, not even the King's counsellors, opened his lips. The two hostile bodies of men eyed one another, wondering, perhaps, whether the next few minutes would see them locked in a bloody struggle. Tyler was baffled, and to hide his indecision, demanded a flagon of ale to quench his thirst – it was a hot day. A man from the ranks of the rebels brought him what he needed, and there, standing within a few paces of the King, he indicated his indifference to majesty and his ill-mannered assumption of equality by swallowing the liquid in one great gulp, tossed the pot back to its bearer, and remounted his patient horse.

Behind the King a seated rider stared at the flushed, surly face of the boorish leader, and exclaimed so loudly that even Tyler heard him: 'I know this fellow. He's the most notorious highwayman and thief of my country.' The speaker was a Kentish servant of the King. Tyler, about to ride back to his own men, turned, detected the retainer who had reviled him, and ordered him angrily to come out, nodding fiercely in his direction. The Kentish man, taking no orders from a rebel, refused to budge.

This was more than Tyler's pride would stomach. He called up his banner-bearing follower, and ordered him to kill the man concerned.

The Kentish man, frightened now, perhaps, cried out that he had done nothing but speak the truth, and ought not be slain for doing so. Tyler's next action was to produce a naked dagger and spur his horse forward until it was pressing into the ranks of the King's followers, his intention obviously to kill the accuser with his own hand.

This was more than Walworth, the hot-tempered loyal Mayor, could stand. He slewed his horse round and butted right across Tyler's path, shouting that by brandishing in the King's presence an unsheathed knife the rebel leader had broken the law, and he, the Mayor, would arrest him. Tyler whipped his knife without a second's hesitation into the Mayor's stomach, but instead of bringing him down, the blow failed. Beneath Walworth's unmilitary robe was the armour of a trained soldier. The dagger made no impression, and before Tyler could recover balance, the Mayor himself had drawn his short curved sword and slashed down at his exposed shoulder. The blade bit through muscle and sinew, and Tyler was forced down until his head slumped on to his horse's neck.

This opportunity was too good to be missed. John Standwick, a squire of the King's troop, drew his sword and passed it twice through the rebel chief's body. Bleeding, stricken, Tyler turned his horse, extricated himself from the ranks of the loyalists, and began to cross the open space, shouting in a dying voice: 'Treason!' as he went. Then, before he could reach his own troops, he lost consciousness, slipped sideways, and rolled off his horse on to the rough ground, a dying man.

[4]

A WAIL OF HORROR and alarm rose from the massed rebels as Tyler lay in his own blood; they raised bows and fingered arrows, determined to avenge this murder of their great leader. The small band of loyalists opposite must have said their prayers. Nothing now, it seemed, could save them from immediate destruction. But a fourteen-year-old boy had other views. With a bravery and rapidity of decision that even today arouse respect, he rode out right into the open space and trotted towards the rebel ranks. Raising his right arm in his boyish, clear voice he exclaimed: 'Sirs, will you shoot your King? I will be your chief and captain, you shall have from me that which you seek. Only follow me into the fields without.'

He waved his hand towards the open fields around St John's, Clerkenwell, to the north of Smithfield, and moved away in that direction at a gentle pace. There were some hesitation; then, as if magnetised by the iron of this royal daring, the rebels began to move after him. The King's company also turned, and for a time they were lapped round by and mingled with the rebels, though a few of them seized the opportunity to slip away, not convinced that the outcome would be favourable. Among these was Walworth, who, convinced that the King was in extreme danger, sped back into the city to collect up all the men he could and return to rescue his King.

Reaching Aldersgate, the Mayor despatched men to summon the aldermen and officers of more than twenty wards, urging them to call up every armed man. The news of Tyler's death and of the peril of their King acted like a catalyst on the citizens, turning faint-hearts into furies. Before many minutes had passed, men were assembling in West-cheap and St Martin's-le-Grand. Sibley, alarmed by this sudden change of fortune, fully aware of what his own fate might be, did his best to stop the rot. He passed from one group to the next, shouting that the King had been killed, and ordering the burgesses to man their walls and close their gates, not to attempt to sally forth into the fields and be cut down by the rebels. His fellow-conspirator, Horne, joined in these attempts, but no attention was paid to either, and inside thirty minutes sufficient forces had been assembled to enable the Mayor to throw open Aldersgate and advance with a powerful army.

Their numbers appear to have totalled some six or seven thousand men, among whom were professional soldiers from the Tower, and the mercenaries who owed allegiance to Sir Robert Knolles. Walworth, who knew Knolles to be a better officer than he, asked him to take command and move forward. The troops fell in, and came in quick time to the fields of Clerkenwell, where, with a ring of smouldering and charred buildings about them, the King and the rebels were still in the throes of a protracted wrangle. No-one has ever discovered what was said and done during those extraordinary moments. Somehow, Richard managed to keep them quiet until at last he saw, emerging from the gates of the city, the pennants and banners of marching men.

Knolles, experienced in warfare, had embarked upon an encircling movement, and before long his lancers had forced their way through the disordered, unregimented insurgents, and with himself at their head, had formed up behind and in support of their King. Some of Richard's advisers were quick to suggest that now was the time to attack and shatter the unprepared rebels. It is to the lasting credit of the young King that he refused to do any such thing. He was a 'gentleman'. The rebels could have killed him at any time during the previous forty-five minutes, but instead they had trusted him, and he would not betray them now. It is said that he answered these unscrupulous advisers by the words: 'three fourths of them have been brought here by fear and threats; I will not let the innocent suffer with the guilty.'

He announced to the assembly that they could go unmolested. Many of these humble, confused men are said to have fallen to the ground like stricken men, among the corn they had flattened, crying to him for mercy for their misdeeds, which the King willingly granted. At once a rush of men from Essex and Hertfordshire scurried from the fields in their proper directions, and London saw them no more. The riff-raff of the London alleys trickled back to their hovels and holes. Only the Kentishmen were left, still in proper order, as if on the parade ground. The King took advantage of this, gave them orders as if he were and had been from the start their appointed leader, and assigning a couple of his knights to take charge of them, told them to make their way through the city and over London Bridge. He gave his word that they should not be harmed, and believing him, they went peaceably back to Southwark, and thence along the Old Kent Road towards their distant homes.

Richard was still on horseback, watching with a grateful heart the breaking up of the once formidable army, when Walworth rode up carrying for his delectation the head of the murdered Tyler. Walworth had spent part of his time in Smithfield hunting for the rebel leader's body, but at first neither he nor his companions could find it. It had vanished from the open space where it had fallen. Inquiry discovered that a number of Tyler's lieutenants had removed the dying man to St Bartholomew's Hospital. Whether he was dead or not when Walworth arrived cannot be said, but the vindictive Mayor burst into the Hospital; he and his companions seized the body and carried it into the square, where they beheaded it as he had beheaded so many others.

Seeing this gruesome relic, Richard commanded that it should be taken to London Bridge, Sudbury's head removed, and Tyler's exposed in its stead. He knighted Walworth on the spot, as well as the two leading officers of the force that had come to his rescue: Nicolas Brember and John Philpott. John Standwick was also made a knight.

Ignorant of the death of their chief and the dispersal of his forces a number of the criminals and rabble from London were still looting and terrorising the inhabitants. During the afternoon the watch began to take matters in hand, and before long most of these rascals were under lock and key. Meantime, leaving Smithfield at last, Richard proceeded to the 'Queen's Wardrobe', where his mother still lodged. She told him what anxiety she had suffered on his behalf throughout that day, to which he replied 'Certes, Madam, I know it well. But now rejoice and praise God, for today I have recovered my heritage that was lost, and the realm of England also.'

With these words, the rebellion ended. The most remarkable fact is that only one man perished on either side during that strange Saturday meeting – Wat Tyler. The 'divinity' that hedged a King was never more clearly exemplified than on the fields of Smithfield on that summer day.

Bibliography

The Governance of England, by Sir John Fortescue, edd by Charles Plummer, M.A., Oxford University Press, 1926.

Victoria History of the County of Sussex.

Memorials of Old Kent, by the Rev. H. Ditchfield and George Clinch, Bemrose, London, 1907.

A History of Rochester, by Frederick Francis Smith, C. W. Daniel Co., London, 1928.

Rochester Bridge 1387–1856, a History of its early years, compiled by M. Janet Becker from the Wardens' Accounts, Constable, London, 1930.

Cambridge Medieval History, Vol. VIII, The close of the Middle Ages, 1936.

Loci e Libro Veritatum, Passages Selected from Gascoigne's Theological Dictionary illustrating the condition of Church and State, 1403–1458. With an Introduction by James E. Thorold Rogers, M.P., Clarendon Press, Oxford, 1881.

Primitive Folk Moots or Open-air Assemblies in Britain, by George Laurence Gomme, F.S.A., Sampson Low, Marston, Searle and Rivington, London, 1880.

Traditions of London Stone. Paper by Henry Charles Coote, F.S.A., printed in Transactions of the London and Middlesex Archaeological Society, for 1878.

History of Kent, Vol. VII, Hasted.

William Shakespeare, *Henry VI, Part II*.

The True Story of Jack Cade, by Joseph Clayton, Frank Palmer, 1909.

The Rebellion of Jack Cade 1450, by Helen M. Lyle, Historical Association, 1950.

The English Rising of 1450, by G. Kriehn, Strassburg, 1892, London, 1904.

Annales Rerum Anglicarum, by William of Worcester, edited by J. Stevenson, London, 1864.

An English Chronicle of the Reign of Richard II, edited by J. S. Davies, London, 1856.

Historical Collections of a Citizen of London, edited by J. Gairdner, 1876.

Introduction to the Paston Letters, London, 1904.

The New Chronicles of England and France, by Robert Fabyan, edited by H. Ellis, London, 1811.

Chronicle of William Gregory, Skinner's Company, Mayor of London, 1451–2.

Three Fifteenth Century Chronicles with Historical Memoranda, by John Stowe, edited by James Gairdner, 1880.

Medieval London, by Sir Walter Besant, Vol. II, Black, 1906.

History of England, J. Franck Bright.

The Brut or the Chronicles of England, from M. S. Rawl. B.171, Bodleian Library, edited by Friedrich W. D. Brill, Kegan Paul, Trench, Trubner & Co., Part II, 1908.

Prejudice and Promise in XVth Century England. The Ford lectures, 1923–24, by C. L. Kingsford, Oxford, Clarendon Press, 1925.

A Chronicle of London, from 1089 to 1483 written in the fifteenth century, from M.S. in British Museum.

Lancaster and York by Sir James H. Ramsay, Clarendon Press, Vol. II, Oxford, 1892.

Illustrations of Jack Cade's Rebellion, from researches in the Guildhall records, by B. Brogden Orridge, F.G.S., with contributions by W. Durrant Cooper, F.S.A., on the rising of Cade and his followers in Kent and Sussex, John Camden Hotten, London, 1869.

The Mirror, 27.2.1827.

Lives of the Archbishops of Canterbury, by Dr T. Hook, Vol. V.

Penguin Guides to Kent and Sussex.

The History of Kent, by Frank W. Jessop.

Kentish Insurrections, in *Memorials of Old Kent*, by G. Clinch, 1907.

Rochester Bridge and Castle, by G. Shepherd, c.1828.

Rochester, a History of, 1928, by F. F. Smith.

An Entire and Complete History of the Boroughs of Great Britain, by Oldfield.

Castles and Cannon: A Study of Early Artillery Fortifications in England, by H. J. St O'Neil, Clarendon Press, Oxford, 1960.

Dictionary of National Biography, 1908.

Chronicle, in M. S. Cott. Vitell. A., xvi.

Paston Letters, Vol. I.

Chronicle of Grey Friars of London, edited by John Gough Nichols, Camden Society, 1852.

Encyclopaedia Britannica, 13th Edition, English History. *Arms and Armour*, London.

Brazenhead the Great, by Maurice Hewlett, Smith Elder & Co., London, 1912.

History of the Weald of Kent, Ashford and London, 1874, Vol. II, Part I.

Chronicle, Ch. XXVI, Westminster 1480–82, by William Caxton, Second Edition (See above under *Chronicle*, M, S. Cott. Vitell.)

A Chronicle of London from 1098 to 1483, edited by Sir Harris Nicolas, 1827, London.

Issues of the Exchequer, being a collection of payments made out of H.M. Revenue, Frederick Devon, 1837.

The New Chronicles of England and France, by Robert Fabyan, edition of 1811, reprinted from Pynson's Edition of 1516.

Surrey Archaeological Collections. On Some of the Ancient Inns of Southwark, by George R. Corner, Vol. II.

Rambles in Sussex, by F. G. Brabant, M.A., 1922.

History and Antiques of the County of Sussex, by Thomas Walker Horsfield, Sussex Press, Lewes, 1835.

Sussex Archaeological Collections, Sussex Archaeological Society, Vol. XVIII, 1866. Participation of Sussex in Cade's Rising, by W. Durrant Cooper, F.S.A.

History of Agriculture and Prices, by Thorold Rogers.

The Third Volume of Chronicles beginning at Duke William, Raphael Holinshed, 1577.

The Commoners of England, by H. Fagan, Lawrence and Wishart Ltd, London, 1958.

Hall's Chronicle, containing the History of England during the reign of Henry IV and the succeeding Monarchs, London, 1809.

Life and Work of the People of England, by Hartley & Elliott, Vol I.

Transactions of the London and Middlesex Archaeological Society, Vol. V, Nichols & Sons, London, and J. Parker, Strand, 1881.

The Political History of England, edited by Wm. Hunt, D.Litt. and Reginald L. Poole, M.A., by Sir Charles Oman, Vol. IV, The History of England from the accession of Richard II to the Death of Richard III, 1377–1845.

History and Antiques of Rochester, by S. Denne.

Political Songs, by Wright.

Original Letters Illustrative of English History, by Henry Ellis, F.R.S., Keeper of M.S.S. in Brit. Museum, London, 1827.

Leland Collection, tom. 1, from a Manuscript Chronicle, Grafton.

Index

238

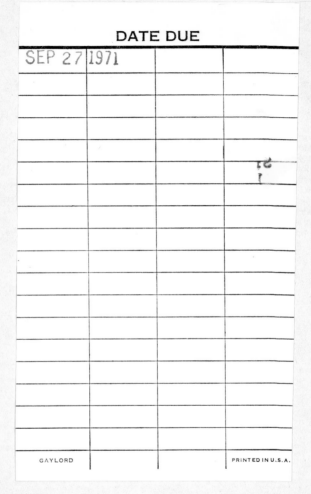

DATE DUE

SEP 27 1971			
GAYLORD			PRINTED IN U.S.A.